◇THE *Teacher's* Guide TO◇

READING

TESTS

D1518042

ROBERT B. COOTER, JR.

◇THE *Teacher's guide* TO◇

READING
TESTS

Edited by

Robert B. Cooter, Jr.
Bowling Green State University

Gorsuch Scarisbrick, Publishers
Scottsdale, Arizona

Dedicated to the memory of Gary W. Bates

Editor: Cydney Capell
Consulting Editor: Alden J. Moe
Production Manager: Carol Hunter
Cover Design: Cynthia Lee Maliwauki
Typesetting: Publication Services

Gorsuch Scarisbrick, Publishers
8233 Via Paseo del Norte, Suite F-400
Scottsdale, AZ 85258

10 9 8 7 6 5 4 3 2 1

ISBN 0-89787-527-3

CONTENTS

JUN 12 1991

PREFACE

Many educators, especially those charged with the responsibility of helping people with reading problems, recognize the great value of accurate diagnostic information. While there are presently some researchers who feel that reading diagnosis should only be performed using informal teacher-devised procedures, the fact is that most assessments, especially in public school settings, rely extensively on commercially prepared instruments. Our purpose is not to debate the efficacy of commercial instruments, but to help educators be better informed consumers.

In order to accomplish our goal, we have three objectives in mind. First, to bring together highly respected individuals in the field of reading assessment to write the various reviews; second, to provide reviews of instruments representing the various genres available to assessment professionals; and third, to provide reviews of many of the most popular and/or controversial instruments presently available.

It is our hope that we have provided a useful tool for those who use assessment instruments. The book can be used as a handy desk reference for reading professionals and as a helpful guide for teachers and prospective teachers enrolled in college courses pertaining to the diagnosis and correction of reading problems. We feel that as teachers develop greater facility in the selection and use of diagnostic instruments in reading there will be a reciprocal benefit to students through better targeted remediation. Thus, it is our ultimate hope that in some way we may help people who presently have reading difficulties to better enjoy the marvelous world of books.

Acknowledgements

I am indebted to the many people who helped make *The Teacher's Guide to Reading Tests* possible. A number of individuals warrant special recognition for their service in this project, for without their help this book would have never been published. Dean Roger Bennett and Dr. Robert Oana of the Bowling Green State University College of Education and Allied Professions have provided unlimited encouragement and support to this project from its inception. Likewise, special thanks are due to Judy Maxey, Sherry Haskins, and Sheryl Sabo, our wonderful staff in the college's word processing center. Their patience with authors is legend! In addition to these fine colleagues, I would like to again thank Jane Sudbrink and John Gorsuch of Gorsuch Scarisbrick, Publishers and Alden J. Moe of Lehigh University. Their confidence in the project and assistance with the manuscript have enabled us to bring to publication the kind of quality product we had all hoped would be created. Naturally, I wish to thank the contributors who entrusted these valuable reviews to my care. Finally, I wish to thank my sweetheart, Deb Cooter, for her never-failing support. I owe her everything.

—R.B.C.

A WORD TO PROFESSORS
OF READING

The Teacher's Guide to Reading Tests, in addition to supplying reading teachers with a useful desk reference, is intended to provide professors of reading with a supplemental text for reading assessment courses. We respectfully suggest that this text might be useful as one of three valuable resources in your assessment course(s) (i.e., your preferred assessment textbook, *The Teacher's Guide to Reading Tests*, and a small collection of assessment instruments). Many professors feel that because this text has utilized some rather functional assessment categories (e.g., Informal Reading Inventories, Group Reading Tests, etc.) it may only be necessary to keep on hand one or two tests from each category for successful classroom demonstrations. Thus, it is hoped that adoption of our text will enable professors to use their resources for other priority instructional items. It is our hope that *The Teacher's Guide to Reading Tests* will be a valuable addition to your professional library. Any suggestions for the improvement of future editions will be very much appreciated.

SOME CONSIDERATIONS IN THE SELECTION OF READING TESTS

The purpose of reading assessment is to provide teachers with an appropriate starting place to begin instruction. That implies not only understanding which reading subskills or abilities students do or do not know, but also knowing something about their background of experiences, subjects for recreational reading that interest them, family reading habits, and students' attitudes about reading. In gaining this important information, reading specialists are confronted with this paradox—we need to gain as much information about the student as possible, but we must never overtest and run the risk of alienating the student.

Perhaps one answer to the paradox is to select tests and diagnostic procedures carefully in order to provide an accurate cross-section of the student's ability. Then the teacher can begin at a logical starting point and attempt to learn what remains unknown through the art of diagnostic teaching. Let us briefly consider two questions that may help reading specialists to construct this kind of reading diagnostic survey.

1. *What do we expect a student of this age and grade placement to be able to do in terms of reading?* Before assessment of any ability can be measured, the "what" of instruction must be determined. Knowing what is to be measured helps us to understand which tests and procedures should be used. For example, a second grade student would be expected to have some knowledge of letter sounds, be able to employ basic phonics skills, comprehend on both literal and inferential levels, and practice basic reading and study skills (e.g., alphabetical order). Thus, an assessment program that samples these abilities is needed. A student in the ninth grade will not usually require an assessment package that samples phonics abilities, but a survey of his or her ability to use such advanced reading and study skills as skimming, scanning, and metacognitive strategies would seem warranted. In either of the above

cases, though, reading attitudes, interests, and motivations should also be considered.

2. *How may we assess these abilities in an economical way?* The "how" question is really two questions in one. First, "How may we assess these abilities" is asking which tests and/or diagnostic procedures should be used to assess the expected abilities identified in question 1. There may be a number of options for the reading specialist to consider. The test reviews in this book were written to assist in that process. It is reasonable to say that there is rarely, if ever, only one best test or procedure for any given circumstance.

The second implied question has to do with "economy." Economy here refers to choosing tests and procedures that require the least amount of assessment time and student discomfort. Thus, the assessment regime should be brief yet thorough. It must provide an appropriate starting place for instruction. It does the reading specialist no good whatever to examine the student thoroughly only to discover that the bond of trust between student and teacher has been destroyed.

In addition to the above questions there are other considerations that apply to the selection of most reading tests. These are briefly examined below.

Validity

The validity question is simply "how well does a test measure what its authors claim it measures?" In truth, no single reading test on the market measures all aspects of reading. Hence, no single reading test may be said to be fully valid. However, that is not to say that many useful reading tests do not exist. Many test makers provide a discussion in their manuals regarding the different forms of validity. Four types of validity commonly presented by test makers are content validity, face validity, concurrent validity, and construct validity. For a brief explanation of each, see the Glossary.

Reliability

Reliability is an indication of how consistently a test measures a given skill. In other words, is the test likely to give the same results today, tomorrow, or next week if it is given to the same person or group? Reliability is usually expressed through the use of a *reliability coefficient* (see Glossary under "reliability"). It is important to note that reliability information is usually made available only for standardized norm-referenced tests.

Pragmatics

There are a few items worth consideration in choosing any test or procedure for reading assessment, which are referred to as "pragmatics." A test may be said to be pragmatically useful if it is easy to administer and score, has an adequate manual, does not take too long to administer, and generally contributes to the building of rapport between the student and teacher.

Special Considerations

Aside from the points mentioned above, there are special considerations for each of the different types of tests reviewed in this book. At the beginning of each section there is a brief introduction which describes unique features and considerations for that test type. It is hoped that these brief discussions will help reading teachers to be wise consumers of commercial reading measures.

List of Contributors

Robert L. Aaron, University of Georgia, Athens, Georgia.
J. Estill Alexander, University of Tennessee, Knoxville, Tennessee.
Marino C. Alvarez, Tennessee State University, Nashville, Tennessee.
Gary W. Bates, Ohio University, Athens, Ohio.
Rita Bean, University of Pittsburgh, Pittsburgh, Pennsylvania.
Don A. Brown, Educational Diagnostics, Littleton, Colorado.
George Canney, University of Idaho, Moscow, Idaho.
Robert B. Cooter, Jr., Bowling Green State University, Bowling Green, Ohio.
E. Sutton Flynt, Pittsburg State University, Pittsburg, Kansas.
Lance M. Gentile, University of North Carolina at Asheville, Asheville, North
    Carolina.
Cindy Gillespie, Ball State University, Muncie, Indiana.
Betty S. Heathington, University of Tennessee, Knoxville, Tennessee.
Mary Jean Herzog, University of Tennessee, Knoxville, Tennessee.
Paul M. Hollingsworth, Brigham Young University, Provo, Utah.
Carol Hopkins, Purdue University, West Lafayette, Indiana.
Jerry L. Johns, Northern Illinois University, Dekalb, Illinois.
Edward E. Paradis, University of Wyoming, Laramie, Wyoming.
Rosemarie J. Park, University of Minnesota, Minneapolis, Minnesota.
Leo W. Pauls, Emporia State University, Emporia, Kansas.
D. Ray Reutzel, Brigham Young University, Provo, Utah.
Victoria J. Risko, George Peabody College of Vanderbilt University, Nashville,
    Tennessee.
Diane J. Sawyer, Syracuse University, Syracuse, New York.
Leo M. Schell, Kansas State University, Manhattan, Kansas.
Rebecca Olson Storlie, University of Minnesota, Minneapolis, Minnesota.
Barbara Wasson, Moorhead State University, Moorhead, Minnesota.

INFORMAL READING INVENTORIES

Introduction

The Informal Reading Inventory (IRI) is generally composed of graded word lists and reading passages. While it is usually individually administered, test makers in recent years have produced IRIs that may be given to groups of students. Emmett A. Betts is generally credited with developing the informal reading inventory in the early 1940s.

There seem to be at least two distinct advantages to using IRIs: holistic assessment of the reading act and a system for analyzing errors or miscues. Students reading whole stories or passages are able to demonstrate to the examiner their ability to "put it all together." Most reading theorists feel that this type of holistic assessment is preferable to earlier "synthetic" assessment models, which break reading apart into its various component skills for examination. The second common feature of IRIs is a systematic procedure for studying student errors as "miscues." Many instruments note such oral reading errors as omissions, repetitions, substitutions, and mispronunciations. Comprehension questions are usually asked after the student has completed the passage.

Several unique features are associated with the IRI. First, because they are "informal," there are no norms tables usually available. Thus, such factors as reliability and standard error cannot be accounted for with any amount of accuracy. Next, IRIs do offer information that is often quite helpful for teachers who use ability grouping—reading levels. They are the approximation of independent (easy or recreational), instructional, and frustration (failure) reading levels. A third characteristic is that the various IRIs reviewed in this text tend to be quite different from each other. That is, beyond the graded passages, they each adhere to slightly different reading assessment criteria, making it difficult to establish a rigorous set of standards for this class of tests. In fact, one might present a convincing argument that classroom teachers could likely construct their own IRIs with as much claim (or more) to validity or reliability as the commercial products.

1

However, several questions might be asked by the consumer that could lead to a logical selection when using commercial IRIs.

1. Is the author's understanding of the reading process compatible with mine and does the test reflect that perspective?
2. Is the content of the passages similar to the content being used for instruction?
3. Would the passages being used appeal to the broad and differing interests of students so that students do not appear to be at their failure level when in fact they are merely bored?
4. If, in fact, the IRI seems to be using a philosophy different from that of the examiner, could it be that the philosophy has merit? If so, why not give it a try?

Analytical Reading Inventory

Authors: Mary Lynn Woods and Alden J. Moe

Publisher: Charles E. Merrill Publishing Company

Edition: Third

Copyright: 1985

Reviewer: Carol J. Hopkins, Purdue University

General Description

The *Analytical Reading Inventory* is an individually administered, informal reading inventory intended for use in grades two through nine. Its purpose is to help teachers identify a reader's independent, instructional, and frustration reading levels and his or her listening level as well as areas of strength and weakness in word recognition and comprehension.

Three equivalent forms of the test, Form A, Form B, and Form C are included, each with their own graded word lists of high frequency words in isolation for the primer through sixth-grade level, and passages with accompanying comprehension questions for the primer through ninth-grade level. Student booklet copies and teacher record copies are provided for each form of the inventory. Criteria for determining the student's accuracy on word recognition and comprehension accompany each passage. Summary sheets for recording and analyzing student performance are included.

The *Analytical Reading Inventory* is intended for use by prospective teachers, classroom teachers, and reading specialists in the observation, recording, and analysis of the reading performance of students in second through ninth grade. According to Woods and Moe (1985), the *Analytical Reading Inventory* "is designed to be used in order to enable the teacher to do the following: (1) identify a general level of word recognition; (2) identify strengths and weaknesses in word recognition skills; (3) examine performance in oral and/or silent reading; (4) examine comprehension strategies; (5) find the independent reading level; (6) find the instructional level; (7) find the frustration level; and (8) find the reading capacity or listening level" (p. 3).

The *Analytical Reading Inventory* contains three forms that are equivalent in terms of content, format, and readability. For example, all sixth-grade selections deal with famous scientists or inventors who developed a life-saving technique or device. Each form of the Analytical Reading Inventory contains seven word lists of 20 words each which correspond to the primer through sixth-grade level. There are also ten graded passages or selections ranging from the primer through ninth-grade level for each form. Individual passages are preceded by an examiner introduction and followed by six or eight comprehension questions. The comprehension questions are categorized as main idea, factual, terminology, cause and effect, inferential, and conclusion questions.

The graded word lists and graded passages are presented in two formats. One, called the Student Booklet, contains only the word lists and passages to be read by the student. In contrast, the other format, referred to as the Teacher Record Pages, includes an advanced organizer or motivational statement identified as the examiner's introduction, provisions for coding the student's oral reading on word lists and passages, comprehension questions and suggested answers, and a scoring guide used to determine whether or not the student should progress to the next passage.

While not a part of the informal reading inventory components per se, the frontmatter of the *Analytical Reading Inventory* contains information for those persons responsible for administering the inventory. Topics dealt with in the section include (1) step-by-step instructions for administering the inventory; (2) the identification and coding of oral reading errors; (3) determining independent, instructional, frustration, and listening levels; (4) quantitative and qualitative error analysis; (5) summarizing and reporting test results; and (6) instructional recommendations based on test results.

Technical Aspects

☐ Passage Content

The authors' objectives for selecting passage content were to prepare nonsexist, original writings that were motivational for both boys and girls. Woods and Moe (1985) state, "the situations depicted in the passages are actions and events corresponding with children's feelings so that the reader may perceive himself or herself in the situation, maintain empathy with the principal character in the selection, or be held by fascination of the mysterious" (p. 5).

☐ Establishment of Reading Levels

Readability formulas and computer analyses of text were used for the grade-level validation of each passage contained in the *Analytical Reading Inventory*. The readability formulas provided grade-level readability estimates, whereas the computer analyses provided information related to vocabulary diversity and syntactic complexity for each passage.

Readability Estimates. Readability estimates for primer through third-grade level passages were calculated by the revised Spache formula. The Harris-Jacobson Formula 2 was used to calculate the readability estimates for the fourth- through ninth-grade passages. The authors include tables which report Spache readability results for primary levels and Harris-Jacobson readability results for intermediate and junior high levels.

Vocabulary Diversity. Realizing that there are a number of factors which determine the extent to which a text is or is not readable, the authors conducted additional analyses of the inventory passages. One of these, vocabulary diversity, is defined as the extent to which the vocabulary items, or words, differ within a text. Factors used to compute a vocabulary diversity score for each passage were the total number of words, the number of different words, and the vocabulary diversity score known as the type-token ratio. This information is reported in table form for all passages included in each form of the inventory.

Syntactic Complexity. Two final measures of passage difficulty reported by the authors are the average sentence length and the length of the longest sentence for all passages. The authors state that by combining information obtained from readability estimates with measures of vocabulary diversity and sentence length, they have demonstrated that the grade levels assigned to the specific passages are valid and that there is consistency within a given grade level for all three test forms.

☐ Field Testing

The *Analytical Reading Inventory* was field tested by having 80 advanced undergraduate students enrolled in reading methods courses administer the test to approximately 200 students in grades two through eight. Particular attention was focused on determining (1) the appropriateness of the administration directions, (2) the motivational appeal of the passages, (3) potential ambiguities in the selections or questions, and (4) the extent to which the comprehension questions were passage dependent.

Conclusions

Informal reading inventories, as a category of informal assessment instruments, are often the subject of criticism. Among the problems noted in prior reviews of the literature dealing with informal reading inventories (Jongsma and Jongsma, 1981; Pikulski and Shanahan, 1982; McKenna, 1983; and Baumann, 1988), are technical considerations surrounding the issues of reliability, content validity, validity of criteria for establishing reading levels, passage content, question selection, and procedures for miscue analysis. Nevertheless, results reported in various research studies have demonstrated that student performance on commercially prepared inventories is generally quite consistent with their performance on other measures of reading ability.

The Woods and Moe *Analytical Reading Inventory* appears to have addressed the concerns raised above as well as, and perhaps better than, the majority of the other commercially prepared informal reading inventories. These authors have made a concerted effort to control the readability of selections, passage content, and question selection. They have clearly explained the criteria for establishing reading levels and the process of developing the inventory. Unlike many other inventories, the *Analytical Reading Inventory* was field-tested with children and revised on the basis of their responses and the suggestions of those who administered the test.

In short, the *Analytical Reading Inventory* is a carefully developed, extremely useful informal assessment instrument which allows the teacher to establish reading levels as well as reading strengths and weaknesses of individual children in grades two through nine.

References

Baumann, J. F. (1988). *Reading assessment: An instructional decision-making perspective.* Columbus, OH: Merrill Publishing Company.

Jongsma, K. S., and Jongsma, E. A. (1981). Test review: Commercial informal reading inventories. *The Reading Teacher* 34, 697–705.

McKenna, M. C. (1983). Informal reading inventories: A review of the issues. *The Reading Teacher* 36, 670–79.

Pikulski, J. J., and Shanahan, T. (1982). Informal reading inventories: A critical analysis. In J. J. Pikulski and T. Shanahan (Eds.), *Approaches to the informal evaluation of reading.* Newark, DE: International Reading Association.

The Bader Reading and Language Inventory

Author: Lois A. Bader

Publisher: Macmillan Publishing Company

Edition: First

Copyright: 1983

Reviewer: Lance M. Gentile, University of North Carolina at Asheville

General Description

The Bader Reading and Language Inventory is a comprehensive assessment battery that is useful in classrooms and clinics to determine reading strengths and weaknesses. It contains a wide range of informal tests including: word recognition lists, graded reading passages, phonics and word analysis tests, spelling tests, cloze tests, visual and auditory discrimination tests, a test of unfinished sentences, an oral language test, and an arithmetic test. There is also a test for evaluating written expression which measures students' handwriting: writing letters and writing words in sentences, near and far-point copying, writing from dictation, and expressing ideas in writing. This section furnishes a Written Language Expression Checklist that can be used to establish a student's profile of writing strengths and weaknesses. *The Inventory* is complete with instructions for administering and interpreting all the tests it contains. In addition, the author has included an appendix presenting three case excerpts depicting differences in cognitive development as a basis for selecting a specific remedial reading approach.

The Inventory was developed for reading specialists, resource teachers, and classroom teachers. The graded passages, which form the major portion of this test battery, are designed to determine appropriate placements of students in instructional materials. No emphasis is placed on determining independent or frustration reading levels. Moreover, since students with reading difficulties frequently have learning problems in other areas, several related informal tests are included in spelling, oral language, arithmetic, visual and auditory discrimination, and written expression.

□ Description of Tests

The Graded Reading Passages range from difficulty levels of preprimer through twelfth grade. They are developed so the examiner can determine an instructional level in word recognition and comprehension. Each level contains three sets of passages. The first set is designated *C*, for children. The content of these passages was drawn from materials used in basal readers at the primary-grade levels, and content area materials for the upper levels. The second set of passages is designated *C/A*, for children, adolescents, or adults. The third set is written at a primary level but is intended for use with adults who are just beginning to learn to read. This set is designated *A*, for adolescents or adults. On the intermediate levels the adult or adolescent passages are designed to assess functional literacy. Beyond the eighth-grade level, all passages measure content area reading skills in subjects such as history, science, art, English, citizenship, etc.

The Word Recognition Tests include graded and supplemental word lists. Each graded word list contains ten words for levels preprimer through high school. Each supplementary word list contains 15 words related to instructional directions, life experiences, and functional literacy. The graded word lists provide the examiner an approximate instructional grade level of reading. These lists serve as the means to place the student at an entry level to the graded passages. The lists also aid the examiner in making some observations relevant to a student's ability to decode words.

The Phonics and Word Analysis tests contain fourteen subtests that assess: letter names, consonant sounds and blends, short and long vowel sounds, reversals, vowel digraphs, blending sounds in syllables, compound words, common prefixes and suffixes, silent letter phonograms, and syllabication.

The Spelling tests are made up of seven individual lists that measure the student's auditory and visual discrimination and memory, cognitive language development, sound-symbol associations, and knowledge of the conventions of spelling.

The Cloze tests are developed to assess the student's knowledge and abilities in semantic, syntactic, and grammatical processing. These can be read to the student or the student may read them. Four tests highlight this section: a cloze test for beginning readers, semantic closure, syntactic closure, and grammatical closure.

The Visual Discrimination tests require the student to match letters, syllables, and words and phrases. There are two tests in this part of *The Inventory*. The first is for nonreaders through grade one. The second is for readers at grade two and above.

The Auditory Discrimination test contains 30 pairs of words that the examiner reads to the student. The student must indicate whether the two words are the same or different. An additional test, Hearing Letter Names in Words, supports the auditory discrimination test. A student who knows the names of the letters can be tested for the ability to distinguish the letter-name sounds as they appear in a word. This skill is useful for beginning readers and represents the student's ability to make specific sound discriminations.

The Unfinished Sentences test contains a series of incomplete sentences that render valuable information concerning the student's interests or concerns. These responses can aid a teacher in developing more personalized reading materials and activities.

The Evaluation of Language Abilities test contains evaluation materials for oral language reception and expression, handwriting, and written language expression.

The Arithmetic test measures the student's skills of addition, subtraction, multiplication, division, fractions, and decimals.

Technical Aspects

The selection and development of the tasks in the *Bader Reading and Language Inventory* were done on the basis of the author's years of experience in individual assessment at the elementary, secondary, and adult levels. The author has also relied on a careful analysis of research and authoritative opinions in the professional literature to create the content of this battery of tests. All sections of *The Inventory* were field-tested using experienced reading specialists with at least a master's degree in reading.

Graded Word Lists. The words for these lists were selected from graded sight-word lists and basal readers deemed appropriate for each level. These lists were tested by having reading specialists record the instructional level at which they had placed students with mild to severe reading difficulties after assessment and trial teaching.

Then each student was given a graded word list that corresponded to the assessed reading instructional level. Sixty-four students were used to validate the graded word lists. Thirty-seven percent of these students were on the same instructional level as the reading specialist's placement. Sixty-eight percent were within one year of this placement. Eighty-seven percent were within two years. Next, the graded word lists and passages were given to 40 students by the author and experienced reading specialists to determine whether these lists could accurately predict the starting point for the graded reading passages. Only ten percent of the time were these lists found to be too difficult as a point of entry to the passages.

Graded Reading Passages. These passages were either written by the author or selected and adapted from materials typical for the grade level designations. Literal comprehension questions accompany each passage and are written to be passage dependent. Inferential comprehension is measured apart from the literal level questions and is not counted in the total reading score.

The Harris-Jacobson and Fry Readability Formulae were used to estimate passage difficulty. Elementary, secondary, and adult students reviewed the passages to assess the content. Those passages students and adults described as unappealing were eliminated.

The graded passages were also examined for equivalence. Elementary students read the *C* and *C/A* passages. Oral reading yielded a correlation coefficient of .80. Silent reading yielded a correlation coefficient of .78. Forty secondary and adult students read the *C/A* and *A* passages. The oral reading coefficient was .83 and the silent reading was .79.

Conclusion

The Bader Reading and Language Inventory is a valuable assessment instrument for reading specialists and resource and classroom teachers. It provides a broader body of diagnostic information than is available to teachers through other commercially published, teacher designed, or basal series developed Informal Reading Inventories (IRIs). *The Bader Inventory* allows teachers to examine the student's spelling, oral language development, auditory and visual discrimination, cognitive development, semantic, syntactic, and grammatical understanding, handwriting, written expression, and arithmetic abilities. It also provides a view of the student's basal reading level, content area reading skills, or functional literacy skills. Finally, the *Bader Inventory* contains a projective series of unfinished sentences to obtain information about the student's social and emotional behavior. Responses to these incomplete sentences may reveal the student's interests and concerns that are vital to diagnosis and remediation in reading.

The expanded content of *Bader's Inventory* encourages a more formidable view of measurement and remediation in reading. Historically, classroom teachers were directed to use IRIs as "tests" that were easy to administer, interpret and score. The emphasis was placed on expedience and ease. This created the notion that teachers need only identify specific skills deficits and an instructional "cure" could easily be fashioned to relieve the symptoms of reading difficulty. Bader's work forges a deeper perspective of reading diagnosis and remediation. It supports the more realistic view of IRIs as assessment instruments, not as "tests" (Estes & Vaughn, 1973; Powell & Dunkeld, 1971). *The Inventory* asks teachers to examine reading in relationship to other skills in language processing, and cognitive and affective development.

Apart from the aforementioned differences, *Bader's Reading and Language Inventory* deviates from other commercially published IRIs in three distinct ways:

1. The Bader examination materials are suitable to the maturity level of all readers, i.e., children, *C*; children, adolescents, and adults, *C/A*; and adults, *A*. Bader (1983, p. 6) explains that this was done, "because the major purpose of graded passage assessment is to place students in graded materials so an attempt was made to create or select and adapt materials similar to those in which the student might be placed."

2. *The Bader Inventory* focuses on determining an instructional level for purposes of placing students in classroom reading materials. The author (1983, p. 8) described this practice by stating, "The purpose of the graded passages is to find the highest instructional level at which the student can comprehend and to analyze oral reading to discover student strengths and problems in reading so that the student can be appropri-

ately placed in materials for instruction. Little seems to be gained by computing frustration and independent levels."

3. *The Bader Inventory* emphasizes measuring comprehension as recall and literal understanding using passage-dependent questions. Bader (1983, p. 6) noted, "Because of problems with passage dependency, inferential reasoning is tested apart from literal recall and not counted in the total score."

While *The Bader Reading and Language Inventory* furnishes teachers an excellent range of examination material there are cautions for using any one instrument to measure reading difficulties. Complete assessment requires the following:

1. *Observation:* to determine the student's behavior toward learning or reading in specific situations and to assess competencies. Teachers should observe the student not only in the classroom during reading or testing but on the playground or in social situations with peers and adults.

2. *Interviews:* with the student, parents, and other teachers to gather information related to the student's educational, social, and physical history; behavior; coping skills; interests; assets; abilities; and incentives for learning. These interviews also help the teacher gain support for intervention from significant others.

3. *Tests:* both standardized achievement tests and informal inventories should be administered to determine skills, strengths and weaknesses, behavior in stressful situations, coping styles, and reading expectancy levels.

4. *Feedback:* to the student, parents, and other school personnel to review the results of assessment and suggest a remediation plan.

Lipson et al., (1984) identified other restrictions regarding IRIs:

An "accurate appraisal" of a child's reading ability can only be ascertained in terms of ranges and conditions, not in terms of grade level appropriateness. While use of any one commercial IRI for purposes of placement seems relatively meaningless, they can be used to gain insight into the complex of behaviors that is reading ability. If reading teachers do not investigate how and under what conditions these behaviors change, they will have missed something crucial about the child's reading abilities, and about the nature of reading comprehension.

The Bader Reading and Language Inventory, when employed as one facet of measurement in reading, can be a helpful resource in establishing patterns of strengths and weaknesses. When teachers take the time to administer and interpret the full range of examination materials in *The Inventory,* it can also provide much broader diagnostic information, heretofore unavailable through other commercially published IRIs. This information makes it possible for teachers to design and carry out effective intervention that produces substantive, long-term gains in students' reading achievement.

References

Bader, L. A. (1983). *Bader Reading and Language Inventory.* New York: Macmillan Publishing Company.

Estes, T., and Vaughn, J. (1973). Reading interest and comprehension: Implications. *The Reading Teacher* 27, 149–53.

Lipson, M.; Cox, C.; Iwankowski, S.; and Simon, M. (1984). Explorations of the interactive nature of reading: Using commercial IRIs to gain insights. *Reading Psychology* 5, 209–18.

Powell, W., and Dunkeld, C. (1971). Validity of the IRI reading levels. *Elementary English,* 48, 637–42.

Classroom Reading Inventory

Author: Nicholas J. Silvaroli

Publisher: William C. Brown

Edition: Fifth

Copyright: 1986

Reviewers: J. Estill Alexander and Mary Jean Herzog
University of Tennessee, Knoxville

General Description

The fifth edition of the *Classroom Reading Inventory* (CRI) is a spiral bound informal reading inventory intended for classroom teachers to use in gathering and diagnostic information about their students' word recognition, comprehension, spelling and listening skills and for use in planning an individualized skills-oriented program in reading. The CRI test can be administered in 12 minutes according to the author.

There are four forms: Forms A and B are designed for use in the elementary grades (1–6) and are interchangeable; Form C is for middle or junior high school students; and Form D is for high school students or adults. Each form contains graded word lists, graded paragraphs for oral reading, and an inventory record for teachers. Additionally, the A and B forms both contain a spelling survey. Information about obtaining independent, instructional, frustration, and listening levels is given.

Technical Aspects

No technical data are included with the CRI. Reliability, validity, and appropriateness for specific populations cannot, therefore, be evaluated. It may be that technical tests to establish reliability and validity were conducted, but if that is the case, the consumer does not have access to that information. The average classroom teacher should be expected to be a critical consumer, capable of critically evaluating instructional materials including tests and inventories before deciding to use or discard the material in question, and should have access to such information. In addition, the basis on which the selection of word lists was made is not clear. It is not known if the words are taken from one of the well-known sight word lists such as the Dolch, Fry, Ekwall, or San Diego. Nor is the selection process from within the lists described. This lack of technical information makes it difficult for the user to know if the recommended procedures are appropriate, valid, and reliable. In reviewing a previous edition (the third), Brown, Phillips, and Colwell (1981) criticized the absence of technical data. The present edition still does not address this criticism.

There are several concerns which arise upon examination of the content and the procedures of the CRI. The students' oral reading selections have illustrations which may influence comprehension, thereby artificially inflating the achieved reading level. Not all commercially produced IRIs contain illustrations. For example, Johnsons' *Basic Reading Inventory* (1985) has been praised for not including pictures because of the problem of artificially inflating the reading level.

Although Dr. Silvaroli states that the comprehension questions are passage-dependent, there are instances in which this is not necessarily the case. (See examples on p. 20, #5 "What does this spider probably eat?"; p. 55, #1, "Name two things birds like to eat."; #3 "What does the word 'grind' mean?"; p. 56, #4, "Why do sky divers need to use airplanes?")

The selections are followed by factual, inferential, and vocabulary questions. The great majority of comprehension questions are factual, however. In light of potential problems created by passage independent questions, the reviewers are not convinced that the question category breakdown will always adequately assess comprehension at lower or higher processing levels.

Administering silent reading passages is not a part of the usual procedure for the CRI. On page three, only oral reading of paragraphs is recommended. In the directions on page four, it is stated that the Graded Oral Paragraphs in Form B may be used as a set of silent paragraphs for students who might reject oral reading or for more complete assessment of overall reading achievement. For teachers with little background in diagnosis, this emphasis on oral reading may lead to the belief that silent reading is not in fact an important part of the procedure for determining reading level and for planning the reading improvement program.

Self-corrections are considered correct on the word lists but not on the oral paragraphs. Dr. Silvaroli gives a justification for this inconsistency, a procedure he refers to as undercutting. He defines undercutting as a procedure for under-estimating a child's reading level to avoid starting the test on a higher, possibly frustrating, level. It would be helpful to know if this undercutting procedure has a theoretical basis. Mispronunciations are not included in the list of common errors (see page nine). Most authors of IRIs give attention to gross and/or partial mispronunciations. Mispronunciations have been found to be among the errors that interfere most with comprehension (Dunkeld, 1970). Silvaroli does not dis-cuss mispronunciations at all.

As a final criticism, the CRI appears to be theoretically aligned with "bottom up" conceptions of the reading process. That is, it is described as a skills oriented reading program. It may lead unsuspecting and inexperienced teachers to think of reading in overly simplistic terms. It might contribute to the erroneous as-sumption that skills add up to reading proficiency.

There are several positive points that may be made about the CRI, however. For example, there seems to have been an attempt to make the content of pas-sages similar at specific levels across forms, which should help with alternate-form reliability.

In addition, the CRI interpretation section (pages 15 through 18) provides useful advice to the teacher. Particularly noteworthy is the recommendation to the teacher to use some references in developing a better understanding of word recognition and comprehension problems and their solutions. Probably one of the most appealing features of the CRI is its efficiency. It is stated that a teacher can give the CRI in 12 minutes. An experienced teacher, with adequate back-ground in reading, who would know how to adapt the CRI for her or his own purposes, may be able to use it effectively as part of a diagnostic procedure.

Conclusions

The CRI is an easy instrument for teachers to use in obtaining information relative to reading levels. However, the most important component of a reading diagnosis, silent reading, is not assessed in the 12 minute time frame. Teachers should consider giving Form B to check silent reading comprehension. It is important for teachers to know whether there are performance differences in silent and oral reading.

But, given the information available from many basal reading assessment programs and commonly used tests, such as the *Metropolitan Achievement Tests: Sixth Edition* (Psychological Corporation, 1985), it is often unnecessary for teachers to use an instrument such as the CRI in order to determine reading levels. Moreover, in light of the criticisms discussed above, when used by an inexperienced teacher with little background in reading theory, the CRI may provide a superficial quantitative type of diagnosis without regard to the qualitative, processing aspects of reading.

References

Brown, O. S.; Phillips, K.; and Colwell, C. G. (1981). Classroom reading inventory. In L. M. Schell, *Diagnostic and criterion-referenced reading tests: Review and evaluation*. Newark, DE: International Reading Association.

Dunkeld, Cohen, G. M. (1970). The validity of the informal reading inventory for the designation of instructional levels: A study of the relationships between children's gains in reading achievement and the difficulty of instructional materials. Unpublished doctoral dissertation, University of Illinois at Urbana-Champaign.

Johns, Jerry L. (1985). *Basic reading inventory* (2nd ed.). Dubuque, IA: Kendall-Hunt.

Diagnostic Reading Scales*

Author: George D. Spache

Publisher: McGraw-Hill

Edition: 1981 Edition

Copyright: 1981

Reviewer: Barbara Wasson, Moorhead State University

General Description

The *Diagnostic Reading Scales* consist of a series of integrated tests which provide standardized evaluations of oral and silent reading skills and of auditory comprehension. In addition, 12 tests of word analysis and phonics are included. Administration requires from 45 minutes to one hour.

The tests are intended for use in determining the reading proficiency of normal and disabled readers at the elementary school level and of disabled readers of junior and senior high school age.

Testing begins with the administration of a word-recognition list. The student's performance on the word-recognition list allows the examiner to estimate the level at which to start the oral reading passages, to discover the methods

---

* Editor's Note: While some may categorize the DRS as an individual diagnostic reading test, it is our view that it has the typical components of an IRI.

a student uses in word attack and analysis and the kinds of errors which are made, and to evaluate the student's sight vocabulary.

In oral paragraph reading, the student's errors and comprehension scores enable the examiner to estimate the most suitable level of instructional materials for the student. The instructional level is determined by noting the number of oral reading errors and the number of comprehension questions answered correctly for each paragraph. Omissions, additions, substitutions, repetitions of two or more words, and reversals are scored as errors. Hesitations, self-corrections or dialectical pronunciations do not count as errors. Comprehension is tested with seven or eight short questions asked of the student, the clear majority of which require literal recall of information found in the paragraph. Excessive oral reading errors *or* insufficient number of comprehension questions answered correctly suggest that the level of reading is too difficult for the child. The most difficult paragraph read with a satisfactory level of oral reading and comprehension accuracy is considered to be the instructional level.

Following oral reading the student begins silent paragraph reading. The independent reading level is the highest level where the student can read with at least 60 percent comprehension. This is the grade level for recreational and supplementary reading at which the child can read silently with satisfactory comprehension, even though some difficulty with word recognition may be experienced according to Spache (1981). The time required to read each of the paragraphs may be used to obtain a rough estimate of the student's silent reading rate.

The potential level, as defined by Spache (1981), represents the grade level to which a student's reading ability may theoretically be raised as a result of appropriate remedial or classroom training. The examiner measures this level by reading passages to the student and asking comprehension questions.

Word analysis and phonics tests are administered as judged appropriate by the examiner. Test users are cautioned that it may not be appropriate to administer these tests to students who read above fourth grade levels, since, at higher levels, phonics skills are no longer related to reading comprehension (Spache, 1981). These tests are essentially criterion referenced.

☐ Description of Subtests and Testing Materials

The test battery includes three word-recognition lists that range in difficulty from the 1.4 to the 5.5 grade level and 22 reading passages of graduated difficulty from the 1.4 to the 7.5 grade level. Comprehension questions with answers (for the examiner) accompany each passage. The following 12 supplementary word analysis and phonics tests are also provided: initial consonants, final consonants, consonant digraphs, consonant blends, initial consonant substitution, initial consonant sounds (recognized auditorily), auditory discrimination, short and long vowel sounds, vowels with *r*, vowel diphthongs and digraphs, common syllables or phonograms, and blending.

The testing materials consist of a reusable spiral bound test book for the student, a record booklet for the examiner's use, and the examiner's manual. The first part of the manual contains a description of the scales. Part two gives directions for administering and scoring the tests. Part three describes the interpretation of results. Data on test development are given in part four. The last pages of the record booklet provide check lists of word analysis skills, use of graphic clues and context clues, and reading ability. A summary record sheet is also included. In addition, an Examiner's Cassette and Technical Report are also available.

Technical Aspects

The 1963 edition of the *Diagnostic Reading Scales* was developed over a period of eight years of research to provide standardized evaluations of oral and silent reading skills and of listening comprehension. The 1972 edition was revised following additional small scale validity and passage consistency research. Nationwide research involving 534 students (grades one through eight) was conducted prior to the 1981 edition. This research provided the basis for reassigning difficulty levels to the reading selections, ensuring accuracy of the word-recognition list placements, establishing reliability of the scales, and establishing internal consistency of the 12 word analysis and phonics tests.

A number of variables including readability measures of the reading selections, classroom reader level, and teacher estimate of reading level of students participating in the study were intercorrelated to establish reading selection levels. Reported correlations between instructional level scores and other variables ranged from .76 to .89. The instructional level test-retest correlation was reported as .89. Satisfactory reliability coefficients of the three word recognition lists were reported as .96, .87, and .91 (Kuder-Richardson formula 21, 1972 data). Adequate internal consistency was demonstrated for the word analysis and phonics tests at the first and second grade level. Above second grade, the tests were too easy to measure differences among most students.

Conclusions

Advantages of the *Diagnostic Reading Scales* include their usefulness in diagnosis of a wide variety of reading strengths and weaknesses of elementary school students as well as disabled readers in both elementary and secondary school. The user is provided with an integrated picture of word recognition proficiencies, oral reading skills, silent reading speed and comprehension, potential level, and various word analysis and phonics skills.

Users should be cautioned that despite efforts to improve standardization, the instructional, independent, and potential levels cannot be taken at face value. The instructional level obtained through testing is often found to be inappropriate for teaching. For students with reading problems there is a serious question whether independent silent reading should be assigned at a difficulty level where the student is achieving at 60 percent comprehension, as is suggested in the examiner's manual. The potential level as determined by a measure of auditory comprehension must be interpreted with extreme care particularly for primary grade children. Also, although the word analysis and phonics tests are clear and uncomplicated, because they employ isolated words (or pseudo words), careful interpretation is needed.

In sum, the *Diagnostic Reading Scales* provide an integrated picture of a wide variety of reading strengths and weaknesses for both elementary and secondary disabled readers. The manual is reasonably clear and proper administration is not unreasonably difficult. Interpretation, however, requires considerable judgment. Training in the administration and especially the interpretation of this standardized diagnostic test is necessary.

References

Lipa, S. (1985). Test review: Diagnostic reading scales. *The Reading Teacher* 38, 664–67.

Spache, G. D. (1981). *Diagnostic reading scales: Examiner's manual.* Monterey, CA: McGraw-Hill.

Spache, G. D. (1982). *Diagnostic reading scales: Technical report.* Monterey, CA: McGraw-Hill.

Ekwall Reading Inventory

Author: Eldon E. Ekwall

Publisher: Allyn and Bacon, Inc.

Edition: Second

Copyright: 1986

Reviewer: Edward E. Paradis, University of Wyoming

General Description

The *Ekwall Reading Inventory* is a representative example of informal reading inventories consisting of graded paragraphs and supplementary tests to assess reading ability. The inventory begins with a discussion of the various tests and the criteria for determining the independent, instructional, and frustration reading levels.

The next major section presents a detailed procedure for implementing the inventory. Specific directions are provided for the preparation, administration, and scoring of the graded word list and the graded reading passages. The last portion of this section introduces instruments to measure phonics word attack skills.

Four separate tests follow, assessing letter recognition, basic sight vocabulary, syllable principles, vowel rules, and contraction knowledge. A flow chart explaining the diagnostic sequence is discussed. The inventory ends with copies of the passages to be read by students and those to be duplicated for teacher use.

The inventory was designed for use by classroom teachers, remedial reading teachers, reading diagnosticians, and school psychologists. In addition the inventory is recommended for the training of prospective and inservice teachers.

□ Test Components

Graded Word List. The *San Diego Quick Assessment* (La Pray & Ross, 1969) is used as the first estimate of the independent, instructional, and frustration reading levels. Lists of ten words each are provided from the preprimer level through grade nine.

Graded Reading Passages. The inventory contains a set of passages ranging in difficulty from the preprimer level through ninth grade. Four passages for each level are included providing an oral reading and a silent reading passage for the initial assessment as well as another oral and silent reading passage should a second test administration be needed. The paragraphs are designed to determine the independent, instructional and frustration reading levels as well as the listening comprehension level. In addition the silent reading rate is determined.

Quick Survey Word List. This instrument was designed to measure knowledge of phonics word attack skills, syllabication, vowel rules, rules for "C," "G," and "Y," and accent generalizations. The list uses invented words as "dawsnite," "gincule," and "glammertickly" for the means of measurement.

El Paso Phonics Survey. This assessment is recommended for students who do not pass the Quick Survey Word List. The phonics survey uses invented words as "nup," "blin," and "tipe" to measure knowledge of initial consonant sounds, initial consonant clusters, vowels, vowel teams, and special letter combinations.

Testing Letter Knowledge. This assessment for prereaders examines ability in writing, naming, identifying and matching letters. Knowledge of both lower and upper case letters is determined.

Ekwall Basic Sight Word Test. This measure provides word lists for the following levels: preprimer, primer, first reader, 2–1, 2–2, and 3–2. Words are untimed in the testing although the instructions recommend counting a word incorrect if the student has an extended pause.

Assessing Knowledge of Syllable Principles and Vowel Rules. This instrument uses invented words as "botnap" or "bashil," requiring the student to explain where the word would be divided into syllables. Vowel rules and rules for "Y" are also measured with invented words as "loc," "nide," and "bly."

Assessing Contraction Knowledge. This test provides a list of contractions representing grade levels 2.9 through 4.5. The student is to pronounce the item and tell the two words forming the contraction.

☐ Diagnostic Sequence Flow Chart

A series of six flow charts graphically portray the order for the testing. The alternative routes through the flow charts are explained by a series of 40 steps with each step usually described in four or five sentences. The first step suggests a short interview before moving on to visual screening in step two, and proceeding to step three where the word list test begins. Following a series of "Pass/Fail" points through the graded passages and the various word identification tests, the final step ends the flow chart with referral to a psychologist. Two brief examples of students' performance on the inventory are included to aid in explaining test administration decisions.

The Diagnostic Sequence Flow Chart portion of the inventory is extensive and detailed. The flow charts, explanation, and two student examples cover 16 pages.

Technical Aspects

☐ The Graded Word List

The original publication of the San Diego Quick Assessment (LaPray & Ross, 1969) did not include information relative to validity or reliability. Ekwall reports that from his experimentation this list has been the most accurate in estimating the independent, instructional, and frustration levels. In addition, a preliminary study with 40 students from grades one through nine was conducted to determine the accuracy with which the graded word list predicted the independent reading level in the graded passages. "The results from this study were that the graded word list predicted the exact independent (entry) level of the student for reading passages 18 percent of the time, within one grade level 28 percent of the time, and within two grade levels 72 percent of the time" (Ekwall, 1986, p. 7).

□ The Graded Passages

Validity for the passages was not addressed specifically in the inventory. An examination of the development procedures for the passages provides information related to content validity.

All passages followed a similar development procedure. The author of the inventory wrote each passage basing the content on research in student interest. Except at the preprimer level, each passage was written using ten sentences enabling the development of ten questions, one for each sentence. Readability level for the passages from preprimer to grade eight was determined with the Harris-Jacobson Readability Formula while the Dale-Chall Readability Formula was used for the ninth grade passage.

Comprehension questions for passages in grades two through nine followed a parallel format. Ten questions were written for each passage with one question measuring vocabulary in context, one question measuring an inference directly related to the story content, and eight questions measuring factual knowledge.

The original passages were field tested with approximately 50 students. Analysis of tape recordings provided information for revising questions. The inventory was then reviewed by colleagues before being administered to approximately 60 students of various ages. Results from these tests were used to make final revisions of a minor nature.

Reliability for the inventory was assessed through an examination of intrascorer consistency. A preliminary study was reported in which 40 students in grades one through nine were administered the oral and silent reading forms and then within a one-week period given the alternate oral and silent reading forms. A single examiner measured grades one through four while a second examiner measured grades five through nine. Product-moment coefficients were calculated for the two oral passages and the two silent passages. For the oral passages, $r = .82$; for the silent passages, $r = .79$.

Time factors on the silent reading passages are included in this edition of the inventory. Slow, medium, or fast reader categories were developed by administering the inventory to approximately 170 students at each grade level. Students were intentionally selected to represent various socioeconomic levels within three school districts. Further explanation of this process was not provided.

Conclusions

The *Ekwall Reading Inventory* is a representative example of informal reading inventories. The core of the inventory is composed of graded passages that are augmented by a series of word identification tests.

□ **Advantages**

The major strengths of the inventory relate to the amount of information gained and the explicit instructions for using the tests.

After administering the eight assessments, the tester will have identified the reader's independent, instructional, and frustration reading levels, as well as the listening comprehension level. Detailed knowledge of word analysis skills will have been gained, including information related to the use of sight words, context clues, consonant sounds, vowel sounds, syllable division, and contractions. The nature of oral reading substitution will have been examined. Comprehension information will have been gathered through factual questions, vocabulary questions, and inference questions. In addition comprehension in oral reading will have been compared to silent reading, amounting to a wealth of information about a reader.

The explicitness of the manual's directions is evident in several instances. One illustration is the explanation for administering the inventory. The sequence for test administration is orderly and detailed, providing thorough directions, such as (1) indicating pages to be reproduced before testing, (2) providing quoted statements for beginning the assessment, and (3) suggesting specific scoring procedures. Further in the manual, the tester is told to laminate certain pages and the type of binder to use. All of these recommendations provide specific direction for the user.

Explaining the use of eight tests and the relationship among the tests can be difficult. This is especially true when the degree of success on one measure determines the next measure. The inventory clearly directs the tester in making these decisions. The series of flow charts and steps of explanation leave little doubt as to the sequence for administering the tests.

□ **Disadvantages**

As is the case with many tests, the advantages of this inventory seem directly related to the disadvantages. The benefits of having a wealth of test information and explicit direction in gathering the data may leave the tester with a sense of having precise knowledge about the individual's ability to read a variety of material in various settings. This belief may be unwarranted. If the concern is primarily to learn about the reader's word recognition and factual comprehension skills in a testing situation, the inventory provides appropriate information. If the concern, however, is to know a student's performance in classroom reading with normal instructional material, the inventory may be of limited value.

Wixon and Lipson (1986) recently discussed reading disabilities from what they termed as an "interactionist perspective." Their concern was that diagnosis using conventional instruments as the *Ekwall Reading Inventory* focused on a search for the cause of disability within the reader rather than specifying the conditions under which a child could learn. Diagnosis in their view should move toward examining the reader's success with different texts while performing various tasks in a variety of settings. This type of diagnosis would begin to identify the necessary conditions for learning to read rather than searching for skill deficiencies within an individual.

A summary sheet in the inventory provides an organization for test results where the user could consider factors related to the reader's success. Category headings as "Oral Reading Errors," "Semantic-Syntactic Abilities," and "Characteristics of the Reader," encourage a qualitative examination of the results. Unfortunately, little direction is provided in the use of the summary sheet. Thus, the tester must rely upon personal knowledge when interpreting the results rather than receive guidance from the inventory manual.

The *Ekwall Reading Inventory* is designed to assess the skills of reading. If measurement of skills is the intent, this is the appropriate test. If information is desired about how a reader might perform outside a testing situation, this inventory will need to be supplemented with data collected in other settings.

References

Ekwall, E. E. (1986). *Ekwall reading inventory.* Boston: Allyn and Bacon.

LaPray, M., and Ross, R. (1969). The graded word list: Quick gauge of reading ability. *Journal of Reading* 12, 305–07.

Wixon, K. K., and Lipson, M. Y. (1986). Reading (dis)ability: An interactionist perspective. In T. E. Raphael (Ed.), *The contexts of school-based literacy* (pp. 131–48). New York: Random House.

Informal Reading Inventory (Third Edition)

Authors: Paul C. Burns and Betty D. Roe

Publisher: Houghton Mifflin Company

Edition: Third

Copyright: 1989

Reviewers: Cindy Gillespie, Ball State University
                Robert Aaron, University of Georgia

The *Informal Reading Inventory* (Third Edition) is composed of a series of graded word lists and graded passages (preprimer through grade twelve), designed to determine the levels of reading material that pupils can read independently (independent level), and with teacher assistance (instructional level). The IRI also helps determine which levels are too difficult for pupils (frustration level) and levels at which pupils should be able to function based on their ability to comprehend material read to them (capacity level). Specific reading problems can also be diagnosed through the use of the *Informal Reading Inventory*. This inventory is intended for use in college-level reading methods classes, elementary and secondary school classrooms, resource rooms, and reading clinics. There have been many changes made from the second to the third edition. The directions and explanations have been rewritten. A case study has also been added to provide assistance in scoring and interpreting. Nineteen new passages have been added and most of the main idea questions have been rewritten.

General Description

The Burns and Roe *Informal Reading Inventory* testing manual is divided into five sections. The first two include background information on the IRI and instructions for its use, including directions for administering, scoring, and interpreting. The background information has been revised to include current thinking about measuring word recognition and comprehension. The directions have been rewritten to facilitate the use of the IRI. The scoring and interpreting sections have also been revised. Sample scoring sheets are numbered to correspond with explanatory material found in the manual. Also new to the third edition is a case study in scoring and interpreting the *Informal Reading Inventory*.

The third section of the manual contains the graded word lists. This section has been revised by placing the student's copy of the graded word list (preprimer through grade twelve) first, followed by the teacher's copy. The words on both Forms A and B, however, have remained the same.

The appendix is the last section of the manual. It consists of information relative to the development of the word lists, graded passages, and new material.

The teacher's form of the graded word lists includes the word lists, spaces for scoring, and the number of errors allotted per level (independent, instructional, and frustration). The teacher's form for the graded passages is conveniently arranged and facilitates scoring. On the left side of the teacher's form is the passage itself. Located in the middle of the form is a running guide for word recognition errors, comprehension errors, and reading rate. The percents have been included to allow a quick assessment of the student's abilities in both word recognition and comprehension. On the right side of the teacher's copy are the comprehension questions, the answers to the questions, and an identification of the question type (main idea, detail, vocabulary, sequence, inference, cause/effect).

The main idea questions have been revised. In the second edition, students were asked to give the passage a title. These questions have been eliminated from the inventory. Generally, there are three types of main idea questions: "What is this story about?" (preprimer through grade five), "What is the main idea of this story?" (grades five through twelve), and "What is the purpose of this story?" (grades four through twelve). Other types of main idea questions are used sparingly. The cause/effect questions are also of two types: detail (directly stated in the passage) and inference. All questions which contain answers not found directly in the text are considered inference questions.

The summary sheet included with the IRI is complete and allows reduction of the diagnostic information to one single page. Space has been provided to indicate the forms used for oral reading, silent reading, and listening comprehension. There are also spaces to indicate the performance levels on the graded passages and the graded word lists. Also included are three charts which summarize the student's performance. The Types of Miscues in Context Chart summarizes the total number of miscues (omission, mispronunciation, substitution, refusal to pronounce, insertion, repetition, reversal), the number of miscues that resulted in a meaning change, and the number of self corrections. The Comprehension Skill Analysis Chart lists the skills (main idea, detail, sequence, cause and effect, inference, and vocabulary) and provides space to indicate the number of questions for each skill type, the number of errors, and the percent of errors. The final chart, the Summary Table of Percentages, allows the examiner to record the obtained percentages for word recognition, oral comprehension, silent comprehension, and the average comprehension score for each level.

On the reverse side is a Miscue Analysis of Phonic and Structural Analysis Skills Chart. Miscues can be tallied for words in isolation and for words in context. There is also an Oral Reading Skills Chart which can be used to characterize students' oral reading behaviors. Finally there are spaces to write a summary of the student's strengths and weaknesses in word recognition and in comprehension.

Two other charts have been included in the third edition. The first is a tally sheet for word recognition miscues. The examiner can indicate the miscues by level and by type. Space has also been provided to indicate whether the miscues resulted in a meaning change and whether the miscues were self-corrected.

The second new chart is the worksheet for qualitative analysis of uncorrected miscues in context. Examiners identify the passage, then write the type of miscue, expected response, or unexpected response. Finally the examiner marks whether the miscue is graphically similar, syntactically acceptable, and/or semantically acceptable.

☐ Description of Subtests

Graded Word Lists. Two lists of 20 words from each reading level (preprimer through grade twelve) are provided. The words selected for each list at each grade level were randomly selected from the vocabulary lists of the Rand Mc-Nally and Scott Foresman series. The graded word lists are designed for making quick approximations of the student's reading level, thus helping determine the starting point for administering the graded passages, for analyzing how the reader attacks words, and for measuring sight vocabulary.

Graded Passages. The factual and fictional passages in the IRI were selected from the Rand McNally, Scott Foresman, Houghton Mifflin, and McGraw-Hill series. Four forms have been included to facilitate pre- and posttesting. The passages range in difficulty from preprimer through grade twelve.

Technical Aspects

Graded Word Lists. After the lists were compiled, each one, with the exceptions of the preprimer and twelfth-grade lists, was administered to students on level, one grade level below, and one grade level above. A word was assigned to the appropriate level if 80 percent or more of the students on level, less than 80 percent from the level below and greater than 80 percent from the level above successfully pronounced the word. Words not meeting these standards were removed and others were tested in the same fashion and added to the lists.

Graded Passages. Passages between 60 and 220 words were chosen from each level (preprimer through twelve) of the Rand McNally, Scott Foresman, McGraw-Hill, and Houghton Mifflin series. The preprimer through third grade passages were checked for readability level using the Spache Readability Formula. The Fry Readability Graph was used for grades four through twelve. Eight questions are provided for each story from preprimer through grade two, and ten questions for grades three through twelve.

☐ Reliability and Validity

No formal reliability and validity evidence is provided in the test manual other than how word lists were developed and how the readability of the passages was determined.

Conclusions

One distinct advantage of the *Informal Reading Inventory* is the inclusion of the tally sheets and the summary sheet. The tally sheets allow students to analyze the miscues both quantitatively and qualitatively. The summary sheet allows for all of the data collected during testing to be condensed to one page which facilitates interpretation of the results. Another advantage of the revised edition is the inclusion of the case study. The teacher's copies of the word lists and graded passages are also an advantage. The teacher can easily check at the bottom of the word list to determine the appropriate level based on the number of student errors. The information provided on the teacher's copy of each passage is also beneficial. Having all of the percents included saves time for the examiner. The questions are categorized by type, rather than literal, interpretive, and analytic, so that a problem with one specific category of questions may be more easily determined. The passages are coded using a series of circles, squares, diamonds, and stars on both the student's and teacher's copy which allows the examiner to keep track of the levels without the student being aware of the level on which she or he is being tested. Generally, the factual and fictional passages containing a variety of subject matter are interesting and appropriate for each level.

The greatest disadvantage of the Burns and Roe *Informal Reading Inventory* is the omission of high-low passages for the second and third grade level. Most all basal series consist of low second and third grade texts and high second and third grade texts. Using this IRI would allow testing of only one of these levels. Therefore, a teacher could not use this inventory to determine whether a student should be placed in a low second grade reader or a high second grade reader. The same holds true for the third grade level.

Other minor disadvantages are the omission of exact readability data and omission of a summary of the types of questions included at each level. Generally, the questions across forms are compatible. (See Table 1 for an analysis of question types. The number represents the number of questions by level and by form.)

Table 1						
PASSAGE	**SPACHE**	**DALE-CHALL**	**FRY**	**RAGOR**	**FLESCH**	**GUNNING-FOG**
PP-A	1.1	5	1.0	3	7	1.1
B	1.3	5	1.0	3	7	1.1
* C	1.4	5	1.0	3	7	1.3
* D	1.6	5	1.0	3	7	1.3
P-A	1.5	5	1.0	3	7	3.2
B	1.4	5	1.0	3	7	2.2
C	1.5	5	1.0	3	7	2.1
D	1.6	5	1.0	3	7	1.8
1-A	1.8	5	1.0	3	7	3.0
* B	1.4	5	1.0	3	7	2.6
C	1.7	5	1.0	3	7	2.8
* D	2.0	5-6	1.0	3	7	2.5
2-A	2.2	5	4.0	3	7	5.6
B	2.2	5	1.0	3	7	3.0
C	2.4	5	6.0	4	7.0	8.0
D	2.2	5-6	2.0	3	7	4.5

PASSAGE	SPACHE	DALE-CHALL	FRY	RAGOR	FLESCH	GUNNING-FOG
3-A	3.1	5-6	4.0	3	7	6.0
B	3.1	5	6.0	6.0	7	6.5
C	3.1	5	5.0	6.0	7	5.6
D	3.1	5-6	4.0	5.0	7	5.1
4-A	3.0	5-6	4.0	5.0	7	5.9
B	3.4	5-6	4.0	4.0	7	5.9
C	3.3	5-6	4.0	5.0	7	6.0
* D	3.0	5	5.0	4.0	7	6.2
*5-A	3.4	5-6	4.0	6.0	7	6.9
* B	2.9	7-8	4.0	3	7	5.8
* C	3.6	5-6	6.0	6.0	7	8.2
* D	3.5	5-6	6.0	6.0	7	8.1
6-A	3.7	5-6	6.0	7.0	7	7.8
* B	3.6	7-8	7.0	7.0	7.0	8.9
* C	3.1	5-6	5.0	4.0	7	7.2
D	3.8	5-6	6.0	6.0	7	9.3
*7-A	-	7-8	8.0	7.0	8.0	11.6
B	-	5-6	7.0	3.0	7.0	11.9
C	-	7-8	7.0	7.0	7.0	10.6
D	4.0	7-8	7.0	7.0	7.0	8.6
*8-A	-	7-8	7.0	7.0	8.0	10.6
B	-	7-8	8.0	10.0	9.0	10.7
C	-	9-10	8.0	9.0	9.0	11.2
* D	-	7-8	9.0	-	9.0	14.2
9-A	-	9-10	9.0	8.0	9.0	10.8
* B	-	9-10	8.0	7.0	9.0	10.7
* C	-	9-10	8.0	8.0	9.0	12.5
* D	-	5-6	8.0	7.0	8.0	11.9
10-A	-	9-10	10.0	-	13-15	20.4
* B	-	7-8	7.0	8.0	9.0	8.7
C	-	9-10	10.0	10.0	11.0	15.8
* D	-	11-12	9.0	9.0	11.0	12.7
*11-A	-	7-8	9.0	9.0	10.0	12.2
* B	-	9-10	9.0	10.0	10.0	13.0
* C	-	13-15	12.0	10.0	13.0	18.1
D	-	11-12	11.0	12.0	13.0	20.8
*12-A	-	11-12	9.0	13.0	11.0	13.9
B	-	11-12	12.0	13.0	13.0	16.0
C	-	9-10	12.0	12.0	13-15	16.1
* D	-	11-12	13.0	13.0	15.0	21.7

Reading Miscue Inventory: Alternative Procedures

Authors: Y. Goodman, D. Watson, and C. Burke

Publisher: Richard C. Owen Publishers, Inc.

Edition: Second

Copyright: 1987

Reviewer: Victoria J. Risko, George Peabody College of Vanderbilt University

In their text, *Reading Miscue Inventory: Alternative Procedures*, Goodman, Watson, and Burke present the theory that supports evaluating oral reading through miscue analysis, four alternate procedures to conduct such an assessment, and the relationship between miscue analysis and instructional planning. The authors establish three purposes for miscue analysis: (1) to help teachers and researchers learn more about the reading process through several levels of analyses of qualitative data, (2) to provide a thorough assessment of an individual student's oral reading strategies, and (3) to use the oral reading data to determine how text characteristics may or may not facilitate the student's use of oral reading strategies. The following review contains a description and an evaluation of the text as it relates to the authors' stated purposes and other assessment factors.

General Description

☐ Theoretical Support

Kenneth Goodman's model of the reading process provides the basis for the use and interpretation of oral reading miscues. As the authors indicate, miscue research has greatly influenced the Goodman model and sustained and extended the use of miscue analysis for assessment and curriculum development. In chapter 2, the authors discuss these four basic assumptions of the Goodman model: (1) reading is a dynamic exchange of meaning, called a "transaction," that occurs between the reader, writer, and text; (2) reading is a language process; (3) readers' knowledge of language affects their reading; and (4) authors' knowledge of language influences how texts are written. Goodman, Watson, and Burke explain that readers and authors are mutually enabling as meaning is constructed by the reader. Reading as a transaction is defined by the simultaneous change that occurs for both the reader and text (e.g., readers add new information to their knowledge base, and text ideas are changed according to the reader's interpretation). Goodman, Watson, and Burke suggest that oral language and reading are parallel systems which have both shared features (syntactic and semantic systems) and unique structures and purposes (an author may write a story following a folk tale genre but orally tell the story using a different structure).

Goodman, Watson, and Burke describe the language cueing systems (graphophonic, syntactic, semantic, and pragmatic) and the reading strategies (initiating and sampling, predicting and confirming) that Kenneth Goodman suggests interrelate during reading and that are assessed during miscue analysis. According to the Goodman model, readers are most able to predict meaning from text when the language and concepts of the reader and author are similar and compatible. The process of how readers initiate, sample, and predict ideas according to their language and knowledge base and how these behaviors lead to confirmation of meaning is discussed.

☐ Alternative Procedures for the Administration of the Inventory

Four alternative procedures are provided for the recording and evaluation of oral miscues and retellings. Procedure I, the most complex procedure, is similar to an earlier version of miscue analysis (Goodman & Burke, 1970). This procedure requires a separate examination of each miscue and the simultaneous analysis of the relationship between the context of the miscue and the reader's language and prior knowledge. After the miscues are recorded on a typescript of the original written text, the miscues are numbered and transferred to a coding sheet. Finally, all data are transferred to a reader's profile or summary form.

The type of miscues that are coded are substitutions (including reversals), omissions, insertions, and intonation shifts that change syntactic structures or the meaning. Similar to the earlier version of the *Reading Miscue Inventory* (1972), all miscues are scored even if they are later corrected. Other miscues that are recorded, but not coded, are used for descriptive purposes. These include repeated miscues (repeated identical miscues), miscues that represent variations due to phonological dialect differences, new miscues made during a correction attempt, and multiple miscues (the first miscue produced is coded, and subsequent miscues on the same text section are recorded but not coded).

Six questions are used to judge semantic and syntactic acceptability, meaning change, the use of self-corrections, graphic and sound similarity, and grammatical function. Different from the other three procedures, partial sentences are examined to provide information about a reader's prediction strategies by judging whether the part of the sentence that precedes or follows the miscue is acceptable.

Another level of analysis is provided through the use of the coding form to identify patterns (meaning construction and grammatical relationships) of a student's proficient use of reading strategies. These patterns are to be considered in relationship to other factors (language background, sociocultural context) that may affect each student's performance.

A guide for scoring the retelling is provided. One hundred points are distributed across story grammar elements for narratives and specific details, generalizations, and major concepts for expository text. The authors suggest a flexible distribution of the retelling points to accommodate factors such as the purpose of testing, the age and interests of the students, and text characteristics.

Procedures II, III, and IV are offered to reduce the time needed to complete the more complex analysis required for Procedure I. In Procedure II, the major focus of the analysis is the sentence within the context of the entire text. Procedure II differs from I by the provision of (1) a simultaneous evaluation of the miscues that occur within the entire sentence, (2) the examination of all sentences that are read whether or not they contain miscues, (3) five questions that are asked during miscue analysis, and (4) the use of an anecdotal scoring of retellings. Questions of syntactic acceptability, semantic acceptability, meaning change, and graphic and sound similarity are used. On the coding form, the miscues are judged according to language sense (whether the reader produces sentences that make sense and sound like language) and word substitutions in context (whether the substitutions are graphically or phonologically similar).

Procedure III provides essentially the same information as Procedure II. The third procedure differs from the second by the use of the right margin of typescript for marking, coding, and analyzing the miscues; and judging of miscues according to four questions to evaluate syntactic and semantic acceptability, meaning change, and graphic similarity. The reader's profile is either summarized on the typescript or a separate profile form is used. Scoring of retellings is the same as advised for Procedure II.

Procedure IV follows the format of an individual reading conference. The miscues are judged according to semantic acceptability and self-correction. Rather than taping the student's reading or recording miscues on a typescript, the examiner keeps a tally of meaningful sentences that are produced while the student is reading. Comments and anecdotal notes are kept on the student's retelling. Because of its abbreviated form, this procedure could be adopted as part of a classroom teacher's routine assessment program.

Four appendices are included to supplement the authors' discussion of assessment procedures. Appendices A, B, C, and D, respectively, provide a summary of each procedure, a miscue analysis for an exemplar, blank scoring forms, and a summary of the previous (1970) miscue analysis format. At the end of the text a list of references are provided for strategy lessons and whole language instruction; background information, theory, and research; and books for children and young adults.

□ Curriculum Development

In Part III of the text, the authors describe whole language reading programs in which listening, reading, and writing strategies "keep the systems of language unified in a mutually supportive way" (p. 109) and facilitate the student's use of prior knowledge to obtain meaning of new information. The authors conclude with a precise description of how an exemplar's oral reading performance was analyzed and then instructional recommendations illustrating how to enhance the student's strengths and minimize his or her weaknesses.

Technical Aspects

The authors present general information about research efforts supporting the use and value of the *Reading Miscue Inventory*. The *Goodman Taxonomy of Reading Miscues* (Goodman, 1973) is used to categorize oral reading miscues and to evaluate how miscues affect reading comprehension. The authors credit the research of Kenneth Goodman and his colleagues for refining the miscue categorization system, adapting procedures, and identifying questions to guide the analysis of miscues. Relying on Kenneth Goodman's theoretical and empirical base, the authors provide no further justification for their definition and categorization of miscues.

The *Reading Miscue Inventory* is not purported to be a standardized test of oral reading and, therefore, the authors do not provide statistical data related to a standardization sample or a set of established stories for students' oral reading. The authors explain that alternative and nonstandardized procedures for administering the inventory allow researchers and teachers to adapt testing procedures and to select materials according to their own diagnostic or instructional setting, purpose, and audience.

The authors provide little information about the technical adequacy of this measure. They offer no empirical evidence for reliability in assessing oral reading miscues and strategies or correlational evidence linking performance on the inventory and successful reading in other contexts. Detailed examples are provided to explain the scoring criteria, but no information is given about inter-scorer reliability. Such inter-scorer reliability may be difficult to establish because examiners are encouraged to assign miscues to more than one linguistic category (see Leu, 1982). Judging miscues according to multiple information sources may decrease consistent interpretations across examiners. Even though the authors advise examiners to use the inventory as a repeated measure (i.e., across varying materials and contexts) to provide a broad sampling base from which instructional decisions can be made, they do not substantiate that repeated administration will provide consistent information. Further, they do not explain how different levels of passage difficulty may affect types of miscues. Information about scoring the retelling is limited in scope, and the authors' suggestion to assign points according to story elements needs further elaboration and examples.

Data concerning the validity of the measure are lacking. For example, information about how treatment of weak areas identified through a miscue analysis will enhance subsequent oral and/or silent reading comprehension problems during reading instruction is needed. More evidence is needed about how the constructs underlying the miscue categories relate to other cognitive and reading constructs and to strategic knowledge and use. No data are presented to demonstrate that performance on this inventory and performance on other reading measures, administered concurrently or at a later time, are associated to any degree.

Evaluation

This text provides significant contributions to the evaluation of oral reading performance through (1) its provision of a theoretical rationale for miscue analysis, (2) the delineation and description of qualitative and quantitative data that can be obtained, and (3) its discussion of how miscue data can be used for curriculum planning. Most authors of oral reading tests provide no theoretical explanation for their choice or evaluation of oral reading behaviors (Allington, 1984; Leu, 1982). The authors of the reading miscue inventory lay the foundation for its use by describing precisely the philosophy that distinguishes their assessment tool from others. As Yetta Goodman (personal communication, 1986) indicates, the meaningful and effective use of miscue analysis requires a careful study of the complex theoretical paradigm that provides support for its use.

The *Reading Miscue Inventory* is the only oral reading test that is based on psycholinguistic theory, and Goodman, Watson, and Burke refer to this theory to provide a rationale for their choice of oral reading strategies, text information sources, and miscue classifications. The authors encourage researchers and teachers to think of miscues as natural aspects of reading acquisition instead of faulty errors that can be studied to learn about the reading process and students' use of oral reading strategies. The simultaneous use of language and meaning strategies is examined rather than considering these as discrete and mutually exclusive behaviors.

Providing four alternative procedures reduces administration and evaluation time, but also serves to broaden the use of miscue analysis. For example, the parsing of sentences (within Procedure I) according to miscue occurrence allows for a precise evaluation of the student's sampling and predicting strategies. In Procedure II, the relationship between sentences that contain miscues and those that do not is examined to determine the effect of miscues on total text reading. Within Procedure IV, the examiner is encouraged to conduct a student interview to investigate how multiple factors (e.g., student interest, text factors) may interrelate to facilitate oral reading performance. Such variations in procedures allow for a multiple and flexible use of miscue analysis.

Assessing comprehension through the use of oral retellings is another strength of the reading miscue analysis. Too often oral reading tests are accompanied with a set of predetermined questions that do not assess students' understanding of central elements of text, students' use of prior knowledge to make inferences (Johnston, 1984), or the student's ability to relate major and supporting details.

With a retelling format, the examiner can determine how students organize the recalled information as they present literal details, relationships among ideas, generalizations, and statement of theme.

The encouragement to evaluate oral reading performance with the use of multiple tests and different instructional contexts establishes the concept that oral reading is not a fixed state and that it is affected by multiple factors. One-shot testing may not test a student's optimal ability across different reading events and purposes (Wixson, 1979) or produce findings that can be generalized to other contexts (e.g., Allington, 1984; Leu, 1982). Assessment findings are more reliable when factors such as complexity of text structure and the student's interests and prior knowledge are considered. The use of full length texts that are similar to the ones used in the students' instructional program contributes also to the ecological validity of the findings.

The description of the whole language curriculum and how it can be used to encourage language- and meaning-based reader strategies is another strength of this text. Rather than providing a list of discrete activities that can be matched to a list of discrete ratio with student weaknesses, the authors suggest global and integrative ways to build on the student's strengths and enhance less proficient strategies. The goal of such instruction is to encourage the reader's development and flexible use of a balanced set of strategies.

The *Reading Miscue Inventory* has several limitations. The most significant limitation is its complex scoring system. Even though the authors present numerous and precise examples of how miscues are judged, the various levels of evaluation pose problems for establishing reliable and valid interpretations. Second, the authors need to present precisely, rather than generally, the empirical evidence that they and others have collected to support their miscue procedures and interpretations, and the technical adequacy of the inventory. Third, the authors continue to recommend that oral reading assessment be used to plan for silent reading instruction and do not acknowledge the concerns (e.g., Leu, 1982) that have been identified about this practice. Since Kenneth Goodman's model assumes that a unitary process affects both oral and silent reading performance, the authors could discuss how their research has influenced their interpretation of oral reading data to generate recommendations for curriculum development.

In conclusion, this text provides a valuable and far-reaching contribution to our understanding of oral reading. The authors' evaluation procedures encourage teachers and researchers to view assessment as a dynamic process (Johnston, 1984) in which multiple measures are used to examine how student, text, and environmental factors interrelate and affect oral reading performance.

References

Allington, R. L. Oral reading. In P. D. Pearson (Ed.), *Handbook of reading research.* (pp. 829–64) New York: Longman.

Goodman, Y. M., and Burke, C. L. (1970). *Reading Miscue Inventory.* New York: Macmillan.

Goodman, K. S. (1973). Miscues: Windows on the reading process. In K. S. Goodman (Ed.), *Miscue analysis: applications to reading instruction.* Urbana, IL: ERIC Clearinghouse on Reading and Communication Skills and the National Council of Teachers of English.

Hood, J. (1975–1976). Qualitative analysis of oral reading errors: The inter-judge reliability of scores. *Reading Research Quarterly* 11, 577–98.

Johnston, P. H. (1984). Assessment in reading. In P. D. Pearson (Ed.), *Handbook of reading research.* (pp. 147–82) New York: Longman.

Leu, D. J. (1982). Oral reading error analysis: A critical review of research and application. *Reading Research Quarterly* 17, 420–37.

Wixson, K. K. (1979). Miscue analysis: A critical review. *Journal of Reading Behavior* 11, 163–75.

Sucher-Allred Group Reading Placement Test

Authors: Floyd Sucher and Ruel A. Allred

Publisher: The Economy Company

Edition: First

Copyright: 1986

Reviewers: Paul M. Hollingsworth and D. Ray Reutzel, Brigham Young University

General Description

The *Sucher-Allred Group Reading Placement Test* is designed to be used in the classroom and administered to a group for initial screening and reading placement. Much like an informal reading inventory, the test is used to determine the instructional reading level for each child. The general format consists of: (1) vocabulary tests of word opposites to check word understanding and (2) silent reading tests of short passages to check reading comprehension. Each section is arranged in ascending levels of difficulty from easy to more difficult.

The test is published in two forms (X and Y). The administration time needed for this test is 40 minutes—10 minutes for orientation and 30 minutes for testing. Scoring is simply done by recording the total number correct on both parts of each subtest. These scores are totaled and a conversion table is used to determine the instructional reading level.

The *Sucher-Allred Group Reading Placement Test* is intended to be used by the classroom teacher to determine the approximate instructional reading levels of students in grades two through twelve. Sucher and Allred (1986) recommend that their new individual informal reading inventory be used with those students who score below grade level to determine a more precise placement and to provide additional diagnostic information on a student's strengths and weaknesses.

Each form (X and Y) of the *Sucher-Allred Group Reading Placement Test* has 13 subtests and each subtest is divided into two parts: (1) word opposites test of vocabulary and (2) silent reading comprehension with 13 different passages.

The word opposite part of the test consists of word lists taken from primer through tenth-grade level basals. This part of the test not only checks for word recognition but for the word meaning as well. There are five words in each list. Following each test word, there are three or four word choices, one of which must be selected as an antonym for the test word.

The silent reading comprehension part of the test consists of 13 short paragraphs ranging in difficulty from primer through tenth-grade levels. After reading the selection, the individual taking the test selects the most correct answer for each of the five comprehension questions. The questions are designed to check five skill categories of comprehension: facts, main ideas, sequences, inferences, and critical (thinking) reading.

Both word lists and stories are arranged into ascending levels of difficulty through subtest 13. Subtest 1 is written at the primer level and subtest 13 is written at approximately the ninth to tenth grade level. Scores from both parts of the test are required to determine the student's instructional reading level.

Technical Aspects

☐ Word Development and Testing

The test words and their opposites were selected from a comprehensive list compiled from five basal reading series, published by Economy, Houghton Mifflin, McMillan, Harcourt Brace Jovanovich, and Holt. The contents of the comprehensive word list were compared with the Carroll Word List, the Francis-Kucera Word List, Johnson Word List and the Allred Spelling List. This comparison helped to refine the final word list used in the test. Finally, words were grouped into grade levels. Before the words could be placed in the test for a particular grade level, the test words and their opposites had to be introduced in three of the five published basal readers at that particular grade level or at an earlier grade level.

Initially 20 or more words and their opposites were selected for each grade level. These words were administered to 25 students at each grade level, two through eight. It was determined which students were at grade level by using an informal reading inventory. It was hypothesized that students should get 80 percent of the word opposites correct at their grade level and 90 percent, or better, below their grade level. Words that were correctly identified by all students at grade level were not included in the final test. Two equivalent word opposites tests were then created for each grade level. Finally, these two equivalent word lists were field-tested using 140 students, 20 at each grade level, two through eight.

□ Silent Reading Passage Development and Testing

Four silent reading passages were selected for each level of the test, primer through tenth grade. Readability levels were determined by the use of the Spache Formula for primer through third grade level and the Dale-Chall Formula was used for fourth through tenth grade level. Some minor changes were made to place each passage at the appropriate level. Five multiple choice questions were developed from each passage selected. The five questions were constructed in order to require the students to: find the main idea, recall detail, place detail in the proper sequence, draw conclusions, and do inferential reasoning. The four passages were tested with 25 students in each of the grades, second through eighth. Individual scores on the silent reading passages for each student were compared with scores on the *Sucher-Allred Reading Placement Inventory*. Certain questions were changed and two test forms were created from the four passages. The revised two passages for each level were administered to ten students at each grade level for final testing and revision.

The final field test scores compared results on the *Sucher-Allred Group Reading Placement Test*, Forms X and Y; *Sucher-Allred Reading Placement Inventory*, Forms A and B; student reading placement from reading passages from the 1986 *Economy Reading Series*; and scores on informal reading inventories from Houghton Mifflin, 1983 Edition; Macmillan 1981-83 *Reading Program*; Harcourt Brace Jovanovich 1983 *Reading Program*; and Holt 1981 *Reading Program*. Pearson correlation coefficients were also computed to compare the *Sucher-Allred Group Reading Placement Test*, Forms X and Y, with the *Iowa Test of Basic Skills*. Table 2 summarizes the results of these comparisons.

Table 2

Intercorrelations Between

Sucher-Allred Group Reading Placement Test

and Other Published Informal Reading

Inventories and Standardized Tests*

PEARSON CORRELATION COEFFICIENTS

	Sucher-Allred Reading Placement Inventory		Sucher-Allred Group Reading Placement Test	Economy Reading Passages 1986	Houghton Mifflin Informal Reading Inventory 1983	Macmillan Informal Reading Inventory 1981-83	Harcourt, Brace Jovanovich Informal Reading Inventory	Holt Informal Reading Inventory 1981	Iowa Test of Basic Skills
	Form A	Form B	Form Y						
Form X	.92	.91	.97	.92	.93	.88	.90	.94	.89
Form Y	.89	.89	—	.91	.93	.86	.88	.93	.90
Form X Male	.90	.90	.98	.91	.94	.88	.88	.93	.90
Form X Female	.95	.94	.95	.95	.93	.87	.93	.94	.89
Form Y Male	.88	.87	—	.90	.93	.88	.87	.92	.90
Form Y Female	.92	.91	—	.92	.92	.83	.90	.93	.92

* Sucher-Allred, Unpublished manuscript, 1985.

Conclusions

The *Sucher-Allred Group Reading Placement Test* is a group administered informal reading inventory. It can be used to screen children in grades two through twelve and place them at their reading instructional levels to the extent that informal reading inventories can place students at their accurate reading instructional levels. The test consists of two parts: word opposites and reading passages. It comes in two forms and can be administered in approximately 40 minutes.

The *Sucher-Allred Group Reading Placement Test* takes the form of a group informal reading inventory. Therefore, it should be used with all the precautions that have been suggested by reading researchers concerning informal reading inventories, such as, the difficulty of assessing prior knowledge and comprehension as well as the text organization and validity of reading levels (Caldwell, 1985; Schell and Hanna, 1981; Ahrendt, 1983). It is suggested that this test be used for initial screening only and that further testing be used for more complete information that might be required for specific children.

References

Ahrendt, K. (1983). A commentary on Shanahan's critique of Killgallon's study: A study of the relationships among certain pupil adjustments in reading situations. In Gentile, L.; Kamil, M.; and Blanchard, J. (Eds.) *Reading research revisited.* Columbus, OH: Charles E. Merrill.

Caldwell, J. A new look at the old informal reading inventory. *The Reading Teacher* 39, 168–73.

Schell, L., and Hanna, G. Can informal reading inventories reveal strengths and weaknesses in comprehension subskills? *The Reading Teacher* 35, 263–68.

Sucher, F., and Allred, R. (1986). *Sucher-Allred Group Reading Placement Test, Teacher's manual.* Oklahoma City, OK: The Economy Company.

INDIVIDUAL DIAGNOSTIC READING TESTS

Introduction

For many decades the individually administered diagnostic reading test has been the keystone of synthetic, bottom-up types of diagnosis. Even though reading research in the 1980s has brought a renewed interest in more holistic forms of assessment, individual diagnostic reading tests continue to be an important part of comprehensive surveys of student reading ability.

As alluded to above, these tests break reading apart into what the test authors feel are the essential reading components or subskills. All tests reviewed in this section have attempted to establish some kind of norms to support claims of reliability and validity. Some, like the recent *Woodcock Reading Mastery Tests–Revised*, have used a fair amount of rigor to establish these norms. Other tests, like the *Durrell Analysis of Reading Difficulty*, have not gone to such impressive lengths.

In sum, these tests tend to be standardized and individually administered, and they tend to use a parts-to-whole reading perspective. Therefore, the following questions might be asked by teachers contemplating using an individual diagnostic reading test.

1. What skills or reading elements are under investigation in this instrument? Are they appropriate for my student?
2. What skills or reading elements are *not* studied in this instrument (validity question)?
3. Are the reliability coefficients adequate?
4. Was this test standardized on a population similar to my student?
5. What can I learn from this test that I cannot learn from other sources?
6. Will the format of this test cause undue stress on my student and contribute to alienation?

Brigance Diagnostic Comprehensive Inventory of Basic Skills

Author: Albert H. Brigance

Publisher: Curriculum Associates

Edition: First

Copyright: 1983

Reviewer: Rita M. Bean, University of Pittsburgh

The *Brigance Diagnostic Comprehensive Inventory of Basic Skills*, at first glance, appears to be aptly named. This large (342 pages), spiral-bound volume, is covered in heavy plastic, and has tabs to divide the 24 sections (22 of which are actual tests). Given that this test is used by many reading specialists and special educators, the opportunity to write a comprehensive review of this test, a much-used tool for developing reading programs for students with instructional difficulties, is appreciated.

General Description

This criterion-referenced test includes sequences for 203 skills for readiness, reading, listening, research and study, spelling, language, and math. According to the manual, users can obtain information on the student's performance from prekindergarten through ninth grade in one or more of these areas, hence the comprehensiveness of the inventory. Tests for 44 of the skills have two forms, which permit pre- and posttesting, and many of the tests can be group administered. Various sections can be separated for ease in handling and administration (probably a good idea, given the size of the volume). The manual contains all necessary test information, from basic information about test format and technical data, to actual tests and test administration directions.

The other essential component of the test is a comprehensive record book to be completed for each student tested. For individual administration, the examiner uses the spiral bound book, which can be opened so that the student views the test page while the examiner sees the directions, questions, and answers on the opposite page.

☐ Use

According to the manual, the test has several basic uses including to identify areas of strength and weakness for each student and to maintain a continuous progress record. Test developers indicate that the inventory, because of its comprehensive list of skills, can be used as an instructional guide. The use of the test as a resource in the writing of individual educational plans (IEPs) is also stressed in the manual.

☐ Test Components

Because of the many subtests in this inventory, this section could go on forever (somewhat like the Inventory itself). However, an attempt is made to highlight the essential components of each language-related subtest.

Readiness. The readiness area contains 31 skills, from basic knowledge of body parts to ability to print various letters. Math skills, as well as language concepts, are assessed. Methods of assessment include interviews, individual and group assessment, and class observations.

Speech. This section contains five skill sequences, one of which is a speech observations checklist that can be used by the teacher. The test author cautions using these sequences to make a clinical assessment of specific speech problems, a legitimate concern given the broad-based, informal nature of the tasks.

Word Recognition/Grade Placement. The student's ability to pronounce words in isolation provides a quick estimate of grade level, to be used to determine (1) whether additional testing should be conducted, (2) a level for initiating other assessments, or (3) grouping for instruction. This section contains lists of ten words from preprimer through grade ten. The student is expected to pronounce at least five of the ten words in a list to go on to the next level. Two forms are included to provide for pre- and posttesting. According to the manual, the word lists are composed of high frequency words that are presented in at least six or more basal reader textbooks identified in the test manual.

Oral Reading. Passages from preprimer through ninth grade level, two forms at each level, can be used to determine the independent reading level of students. According to the manual, vocabulary was controlled in the preprimer through sixth grade levels, by sampling "some" of the vocabulary from eight or more selected basal reading texts. Readability for preprimer through sixth grade levels was calculated using the Fry Technique; The Dale Index was used for grades seven through nine. The student's score on the Word Recognition Test is used to determine the initial level when administering this subtest; criterion for passing is for the student to read orally the passage with 97 percent accuracy. There is no measure of comprehension in this section.

Reading Comprehension. This subtest has two components. The Reading Vocabulary Comprehension grade placement assessment consists of three lists of five words each for grade levels one through eight, and is used to measure a student's reading vocabulary comprehension level. The student is asked to identify the word that does not belong in each list. The Reading Comprehension assessment component consists of passages (two forms at each level), primer through ninth grade, followed by five comprehension questions. Students read each passage silently and then respond to the comprehension questions. Questions at preprimer through upper first grade levels are recall, while questions for passages for the lower-second grade through ninth grade levels are multiple-choice questions. Questions generally include several pertaining to details in the passage, a sequence question, one dealing with vocabulary, and one pertaining to the main idea of the passage.

Word Analysis. The word analysis section contains skill sequences for 17 skills. All but one test must be administered individually. Brigance lists the basals that were "researched" in compiling and sequencing the skills included in this section. The term "comprehensive" certainly suits this section—auditory discrimination, knowledge of initial and final consonants, vowel sounds (long and short), consonant blends, digraphs, common endings, vowel digraphs and diphthongs, suffixes, prefixes, syllabication, and ability to read words with phonetic irregularities—are all tested. In testing a student, the examiner will need to observe Brigance's caution that only selected tests should be administered at any one time. Because the tests are assessing skills in isolation, their use in judging the student's ability to apply skills is also limited.

Functional Word Recognition. The purpose of this subtest is to determine if students recognize common words that frequently appear in print. The nine skill sequences include basic sight vocabulary, direction words, contractions, abbreviations, warning and safety signs, informational signs, warning labels, food labels, and number words. Basic sight words have been referenced to various basals and to well-known word lists.

Listening. The listening subtest contains 18 skill sequences, and includes, like the Speech Subtest, a listening observations checklist. All tests, except the checklist, require individual administration. In addition to an auditory discrimination test, a sentence memory test, an oral directions test, and a listening vocabulary comprehension test, this section includes passages to which students must listen and then answer comprehension questions.

Spelling. The spelling section, which contains a spelling grade placement, is designed to provide a quick assessment of grade level in spelling, identify basic word analysis skills that the student can apply to spell words, and identify words of high use (number words, etc.) that the student can spell. The spelling words in several of the subtests are referenced to various spelling programs listed in the manual.

Writing. The writing subsection is designed to determine legibility of students' handwriting and to provide additional diagnostic information. Handwriting criteria and samples are provided in the manual to assist the examiner in identifying problems.

Reference Skills. The purpose of the eight assessments in this section is to determine the student's competency in skills basic to locating and organizing information. Skills include: alphabetizing; outlining; and use of encyclopedia, card catalog, index, dictionary, and parts of a book.

Graphs and Maps. The student's mastery of basic skills for reading and interpreting information in graphic representations is assessed. According to the manual, the skills sequence was determined by analyzing seven social studies programs.

Note: There are ten math tests in this manual, the first of which is a math grade placement inventory. Other assessments include: numbers, number facts, computation of whole numbers, fractions and mixed numbers, decimals, percents, measurements, metrics, and math vocabulary.

Technical Aspects

Overall, the technical data for this test are weak or missing. Although the author indicates that this edition was field tested and lists the personnel and programs involved, there is no indication of how results and comments from this effort were used to make item selections, nor what changes were made from previous editions. The fact that the items in the test are referenced to well-known textbooks is another effort to establish content validity. However, there is no specific information as to how this was accomplished. Given the diversity in basal texts, it would be difficult for a user to know whether the Brigance correlated well with any one basal. Specific information about the referencing of the test to the textbooks would have been extremely helpful to test users.

Although there is an attempt to establish content validity, there is no information about the adequacy of the items in each subtest or domain area, thus reducing the technical quality of the test. Further, there is no mention of reliability. Yet, given the fact that the test has two forms for 44 subtests, which, according to Brigance, can be used as equivalent forms, there should be data to ensure at least alternative form reliability.

A serious problem exists with criteria for test cutoff scores. These scores differ, from one subtest to another (e.g., 50 percent for passing in the Word Recognition Test, 80 percent in the Comprehension Test, unless two forms are used in which case 70 percent then becomes the criterion), yet there is no indication as to how these criteria were established.

Also, although users can obtain grade placement scores for various subtests, it is not clear as to how these scores were determined. Brigance does caution users about using grade scores for more than a holistic picture of a student's reading performance and suggests that other measures, besides the grade score, be used in making decisions about placement in reading materials.

The inclusion of a more comprehensive description of technical data would help users feel more confident about using this instrument both for assessment of skills and as an instructional guide.

Conclusions

In summarizing the strengths and weaknesses of this test, an article by Tuinman (1978) comes to mind which describes some concerns about criterion-referenced measures. He describes the attempt by a tribe of penguins to learn to fly, and the objectives they finally develop after observing the behaviors of various flying animals. His description of their unsuccessful training program, in which they learn to run at great speeds and produce loud whirring sounds (in imitating the largest of birds, the airplanes) should remind us of the limitations of criterion-referenced measures and the need to use them cautiously. Specifically, the selection of items for the test must be conceptually sound; otherwise, there may be little or no relationship between ability to perform on the test and the desired behavior.

The *Comprehensive Inventory of Basic Skills* (CIBS), if used selectively as suggested by the author, can be a helpful tool to the reading specialist, special educator, psychologist, or other educators responsible for identifying specific skill needs and students' mastery of those skills. The comprehensiveness of the test makes it a helpful reference book, to which a professional can turn for a quick overview of a given area, with the knowledge that different measures or additional diagnosis may be essential. The test appears to have great appeal to special educators who must write individual educational plans (IEPs) for each of their students, and indeed, the test developers recommend strongly the use of the test for this purpose. The comprehensive record booklet can be used easily to record a student's performance and to identify skills for instruction.

However, test users must be sophisticated enough to critically assess the test hierarchy suggested in the CIBS to determine whether it reflects their curriculum beliefs about the reading skills that students must acquire to become proficient readers. Moreover, the comprehensiveness of that test serves also as a limitation, in that unsophisticated users may think that the test provides "all that one needs to know" about a student's performance in identified areas.

In summary, the test can be a helpful tool for those using an objectives-based curriculum in which the hierarchy identified by Brigance is accepted, or for those who need to conduct a quick screening in a given area. The lack of technical data about item quality, criteria for standards for cutoff scores, validity, and reliability, however, limit the usability of the test. Educators using this test should, therefore, be aware of its limitations in making decisions about a student's reading performance.

References

Mills, C. N. (1985). Review of Brigance Diagnostic Comprehensive Inventory of Basic Skills. In J. V. Mitchell, Jr. (Ed.), *The ninth mental measurements yearbook* (pp. 213–14). Lincoln, NE: The University of Nebraska Press.

Swerdlik, M. E. (1985). Review of Brigance Diagnostic Comprehensive Inventory of Basic Skills. In J. V. Mitchell, Jr. (Ed.), *The ninth mental measurements yearbook* (pp. 214–15). Lincoln, NE: The University of Nebraska Press.

Tuinman, J. J. (1978). Criterion referenced measurement in a norm referenced context. In S. J. Samuels (Ed.), *What research has to say about reading instruction* (pp. 165–73). Newark, DE: International Reading Association.

Decoding Skills Test

Authors: E. Richardson and B. DiBenedetto

Publisher: York Press

Edition: First

Copyright: 1985

Reviewer: Diane J. Sawyer, Syracuse University

General Description

The *Decoding Skills Test* (DST) is an individually administered instrument that was developed with two goals in mind: (1) to identify children with developmental dyslexia, and (2) to provide a profile of decoding skills that could be used by researchers to test specific hypotheses about dyslexia (Richardson, 1985, p. 279). Despite its intended use as a research tool, the DST is a valuable addition to the range of diagnostic tools currently available to assess the various aspects of decoding competencies.

The DST consists of three subtests: Basal Vocabulary, Phonic Patterns, and Contextual Decoding. Subtest I, Basal Vocabulary, assesses a child's recognition of words that are typically taught (the core or basic vocabulary) in most basal reading programs. Eleven lists of ten words each are included. Each list is considered to be a sampling of the vocabulary taught at succeeding basal reader levels from the preprimer level through the second half of fifth grade. Subtest I yields an estimate of an instructional reading level and a frustration level.

Subtest II, Phonic Patterns, assesses a child's ability to use vowel, consonant, and syllabic patterns to decode words. Six lists of five real monosyllabic words and six lists of five nonsense monosyllabic words are provided to examine the decoding of increasingly complex consonant-vowel spelling patterns, cvc to ccvvcc. The decoding of polysyllabic words is similarly assessed. Again, six lists of five real words and six lists of five nonsense words are provided. Each list is illustrative of a different spelling pattern for the target syllable and those patterns are identical to the patterns assessed for the monosyllabic words.

For both the monosyllabic and polysyllabic words, the nonsense words were created by changing the spelling of one or two parts of each real word presented (e.g., bit-jit, choice-froice; announcer-azzounder). The lists of real words are presented first (monosyllabic followed by polysyllabic). The lists of nonsense words are presented next (monosyllabic followed by polysyllabic) and are intended to provide an opportunity to examine transfer of decoding abilities, observed in the face of real words, to nonsense words. Nonsense words have been found to be generally more difficult for poor readers. Subtest II yields a Phonic Transfer Index (PTI) that is useful in inferring the extent to which apparent phonic knowledge may be automatically applied.

The real words on each of the 12 lists are hierarchically arranged according to grade level of difficulty (Harris and Jacobson, 1972) with the first word drawn from second grade lists, the second drawn from third grade lists and so on through the fifth word which was drawn from sixth grade lists. The authors state that no first grade words were included because at that level most words are memorized as sight words. Recognition of words so learned would provide little insight into decoding abilities (DST manual, p. 4).

Subtest III, Contextual Decoding, consists of eleven passages corresponding to eleven basal reader levels (preprimer through the second half of fifth grade). These passages were specially written for the DST using the Harris-Jacobson (1972) graded word lists. Independent analyses of basal reader passages were undertaken to ensure that the text features of these passages, such as sentence length, number of clauses, syntactic arrangements, etc., were representative of typical instructional materials at each level. Embedded in each passage are the ten words presented in Subtest I for the corresponding reader level as well as six of the 12 words from Subtest II corresponding to the reader level that is one level above the designated level of the passage. All other words in a given passage were selected from lists (Harris and Jacobson, 1972) that were below the grade level designation for that passage. Decoding responses are thus observed twice for the same words, once in isolation and once in context, permitting examination of the effect of context on decoding behavior.

These passages are also used to assess comprehension, reading rate, and error rate. The last two indices are intended as measures of oral fluency. Five literal level questions are provided for each passage beyond the preprimer level. As with Subtest I, Subtest III yields instructional and frustration reading level estimates.

□ Testing Materials

Effective administration and scoring of the DST requires familiarity with five distinct pieces of material—the Manual, the Presentation Book, the Scoring Booklet, the Basal/Ceiling Key, and the Phonic Profile Worksheet. The clearly written manual provides step-by-step directions for administration, scoring, and interpretation. Four test profiles, resulting from administrations of the DST to children in grades two through seven, provide helpful models for interpreting test performance into diagnostic statements and instruction recommendations.

The Presentation Book contains the word lists and passages that are to be read by the examinee as well as brief statements of general instruction for the examiner. The pages are spiral bound, durable, and easy to turn. The cover is designed to yield an easel-like stand to support the pages for viewing from either side.

The Scoring Booklet offers the examiner a place to note errors on each of the subtests and to calculate scores. Significant information from each subtest may be summarized in the Diagnostic Score Summary which appears on the front cover.

The Basal/Ceiling Key is intended to serve as a quick reference for an examiner to consult, if needed, *during* administration of the test. It contains a *brief* summary of the key points to remember in deciding where to begin and when to end testing for each subtest. The reverse side contains examples of notations (symbols) to use in coding the oral reading behavior exhibited on the passages.

The Phonic Profile Worksheet is designed to aid analysis of responses to the real and nonsense word lists presented in Subtest II. This analysis yields information concerning relative strengths and weaknesses.

Technical Aspects

The reliability and validity of the DST have been determined for three samples of children—an entire school building in New York City (N = 238), a Project Follow-Through sample in Atlanta (N = 1,231), and three studies of good and poor readers (N = 300) (Richardson, 1985). Split-half reliability coefficients and estimates of internal consistency (Cronbach Alphas and Guttman Lambdas) range between .97 and .99 for Subtests I and II. Since the vocabulary words appearing on Subtest I are encountered again on Subtest III, the authors considered performance on the two subtests as an estimate of test-retest reliability. All correlations obtained for the total scores and the grade equivalent scores were greater than .97. An investigation of pretest-posttest correlations (October and April) for the New York City sample yielded coefficients of .96 for the total score of Subtest I and .94 for the grade equivalent scores. Pre/posttest correlations for the Subtest II total yielded a coefficient of .90 (.88 for real words; .85 for nonsense words). Coefficients obtained for Subtest III ranged from .92 for the grade equivalent scores to .95 for the total. All estimates of reliability are within the acceptable range.

The DST is criterion-referenced to the reading curriculum. That is, test items were selected to represent specific words and decoding skills taught at precisely designated time points (early or late in a school year) across 10 different basal series representing widely differing philosophies about how reading instruction ought to proceed. If the DST is a valid measure of decoding ability, one would expect high correlations between performance on the DST and placement in leveled books of various basal reading series as well as with word recognition achievement on standardized tests of reading. Richardson (1985) reports correlations of .83 (Subtest II) to .93 (Subtest III) with actual student placement in readers and correlations of .76 (Subtest II) to .82 (Subtest III) on the vocabulary subtest of the Iowa Test of Basic Skills (a word recognition task). Additional statistical analyses (regression analysis) show that phonic transfer, as calculated from performance on Subtest II, is a significant predictor of subsequent performance on the DST as well as of future placement in leveled books of a basal series. The phonic transfer index (PTI) accounts for a significant amount of variance in these two criterion variables, over and above three other predictor variables entered into the equation earlier (a pretest measure of reading achievement, grade placement, and scores on a math subtest of the ITBS).

The DST has been shown to be a reliable and valid measure of decoding ability as well as a valid index of ability to meet the decoding demands of typical basal reader materials, preprimer through grade five.

Conclusions

The DST appears to be a valuable tool for examining decoding competencies. It was carefully designed to reflect the sequence of typical instruction as well as to compare performance on words in isolation to words in context. It further permits comparison of decoding competence for meaningful words to decoding nonsense words. The design of the DST permits test-taking behavior and scores to be compared within and across subtests thus enabling clinicians and researchers to draw more valid conclusions about individual strengths and weaknesses than was previously possible using other tests of decoding ability.

In school settings, the DST might be used as a screening tool to assess the status of students transferring into a system, for screening adults entering basic literacy classes, and for use by psychologists in estimating reading achievement status. However, when an estimated instructional level is obtained, examination of comprehension abilities should be pursued using the texts and mastery tests provided for the basal series or other instructional materials that will be used, before placing a student in an instructional group. The DST's greatest value to school personnel, however, seems to lie in its use as a tool to evaluate the status and decoding skill deficiencies of students known to be having difficulty in reading. If a decoding disability is confirmed, information derived from the DST may be used to establish instructional goals. For example, if word recognition is weak (Subtest I) and is not substantially aided by context clues (Subtest III), energies should be focused on acquiring the core vocabulary of the basal series in use. Similarly, if word recognition is adequate but phonic analysis (Subtest II) is weak, energies should be devoted to mastery of the phonic generalizations presented in earlier books of the basal series in use. Those reading teachers and clinicians who are fairly sophisticated in the interpretation of reading test behaviors will be able to glean more information from the DST than those who are accustomed to looking only at scores.

Of course, some severe reading disabilities are resistive to "common sense" instructional modifications such as those suggested above. While future research using the DST may help to shed light on the nature of these learning problems, DST scores and behaviors, in and of themselves, will provide little insight into such problems.

The greatest potential value of the DST lies in its use among reading researchers who typically work in different sites reflecting different instructional programs. As a consequence of routinely using the same test of reading status across a wide range of studies, researchers may eventually be able to tie particular kinds of decoding behavior patterns to descriptions of disabled readers at different age or grade levels as well as to possible processing anomalies, maturational characteristics, or any of the range of factors that may be causally related to reading disabilities.

The DST has the potential to contribute much to the field of reading if users recognize both its limitations and its richness.

References

Harris, H. J., and Jacobson, M. D. (1972). *Basic elementary reading vocabularies.* New York: Macmillan.

Richardson, E. (1985). The reliability, validity and flexibility of the Decoding Skills Test for reading research. In D. B. Gray and J. F. Kavanagh (Eds.), *Biobehavioral measures of dyslexia.* Parkton, MD: York Press, Inc.

Durrell Analysis of Reading Difficulty

Authors: Donald D. Durrell and Jane H. Catterson

Publisher: The Psychological Corporation

Edition: Third

Copyright: 1980

Reviewer: Jerry L. Johns, Northern Illinois University

General Description

The *Durrell Analysis of Reading Difficulty* (DARD), first published for general use in 1937, has been used for over half a century. This individually administered diagnostic reading test covers a range in reading ability from the nonreader to the sixth grade and is intended primarily for use with students in grades one through six. The DARD consists of tests and situations in which the teacher or examiner can observe various aspects of the student's reading behavior.

The primary purposes of the DARD "are to estimate the general level of reading achievement and to discover weaknesses and faulty reading habits that may be corrected in a remedial program" (Durrell & Catterson, 1980, p. 11). Materials that comprise the DARD include the following:

1. A manual of Directions that provides procedures to be used in administering the tests, instructions for scoring the tests, suggestions for remedial plans, and standardization information.
2. A reusable, spiral-bound booklet that contains passages for Oral Reading, Silent Reading, and Listening Comprehension tests. Stimulus materials used in certain phonics tests and prereading phonic abilities are also included in the booklet.
3. A tachistoscope (quick exposure device) with accompanying cards for assessing Word Recognition and Word Analysis, Visual Memory of Words, and Naming, Identifying, and Matching Letters.
4. An Individual Record Booklet in which all responses are recorded. The booklet also includes a Check List of Instructional Needs, General History Data, and a Profile Chart. Norms for the various tests are in the Individual Record Booklet.

☐ Tests Comprising the DARD

The DARD permits the observation and evaluation of many reading abilities and behaviors associated with reading. Users familiar with earlier editions of the DARD will note many similarities since the structure of the DARD remains essentially unchanged. There are, however, new measures of listening vocabulary and prereading abilities. The various tests will be described in the remainder of this section.

Oral Reading. Eight paragraphs (five primary and three intermediate) with literal comprehension questions are used to provide an estimate of the student's instructional reading level. Provisions for timing the student's oral reading and observing reading behavior in the areas of fluence, word skills, voice, enunciation, expression, and general reading habits are also included.

Silent Reading. Eight paragraphs, equivalent in difficulty to the passages used for oral reading, with provisions for recording unaided recall are used to provide an estimate of the student's independent reading level. Provisions for timing the student's reading and marking a checklist of difficulties (recall, mechanics of silent reading, imagery, comparison with oral reading, and listening comprehension) are also included.

Listening Comprehension. Six graded paragraphs with literal comprehension questions can be used to estimate the student's capacity or listening level.

Word Recognition/Word Analysis. A tachistoscope and word cards (one list for first grade and three lists for grades two through six) containing 25 words each, provide opportunities for assessing the student's ability to recognize words at sight and to analyze words not known at sight. Norms and check lists are provided.

Listening Vocabulary. This test assesses the student's listening vocabulary by having the student assign a spoken word to one of the three categories. For example, the student hears the word *red* and is asked to assign it to the time, big, or color category. Grade norms are provided; moreover, since the same words are also used in the Word Recognition/Word Analysis test, the examiner is able to compare the number of words in the listening vocabulary to the number of words recognized in the word lists.

Sounds in Isolation. Identified as Pronunciation of Word Elements in the Manual, these tests determine the student's ability to give the sounds associated with 16 letters (all consonants), 16 blends and digraphs, 20 phonograms (word families), 8 prefixes, and 8 suffixes. Norms are provided for each type of word element.

Spelling. Spelling lists of 20 words for the primary grades and 20 words for the intermediate grades are provided, along with norms and check lists to evaluate the student's handwriting and type of spelling difficulties.

Visual Memory of Words. For students in the primary grades, 20 letters or words are flashed with a tachistoscope, and students identify the letter or word in the Individual Record Booklet. Students in the intermediate grades are asked to write words from memory after each has been shown for about three seconds. A check list and norms for both tests are included.

Identifying Sounds in Words. Identified as Auditory Analysis of Words and Word Elements in the Manual, this test assesses a student's ability to discriminate among phonemes (sounds) in words and to identify the graphemes (letters) that represent them. After a word is pronounced by the examiner, the student is asked to circle one of three words that begins, ends, or begins and ends like the word pronounced. Norms are provided for primary grades.

Prereading Phonics Abilities. The tests comprising this section assess abilities related to success in learning to read. Syntax Matching assesses the student's ability to recognize separate words in spoken sentences and then match them to words in print. Identifying Letter Names in Spoken Words assesses the student's ability to name the letter (not sound) at the beginning of spoken words. Identifying Phonemes in Spoken Words assesses the student's ability to name the sound (phoneme) at the beginning of spoken words. Naming Lower-Case Letters assesses the student's ability to name letters from printed words. Writing Letters from Dictation assesses the student's ability to write each of the 26 letters in the alphabet. Writing from Copy assesses the student's ability to copy four words. The student can look at each stimulus word while copying it. Naming Letters assesses the student's ability to name the 26 uppercase letters of the alphabet. Identifying Letters Named assesses the student's ability to point to a letter named from among four choices. Both uppercase and lowercase letters are included. With the exception of the last two tests, norms based on spring administration of the tests are provided.

In addition to the above tests, there are eight supplementary paragraphs that are equal in difficulty to the oral and silent reading paragraphs. The supplementary paragraphs can be used for retesting, checking speed of handwriting from copy, written recall, or in place of an oral or silent paragraph that may have been spoiled.

☐ General Testing Suggestions

The testing situation should be casual, pleasant, and friendly. Testing should take place in a quiet room with adequate lighting. Although the tests may be given in any order, the authors recommend use of the Oral Reading and Word Recognition/Word Analysis tests early since the student's performance on these tests will often influence the other tests that are administered. Since some of the tests require accurate timing, a stopwatch is recommended. The student's responses to the various tests are recorded in the Individual Record Booklet.

The general nature of the DARD seems to require an examiner who has carefully studied the manual and the specific directions for administering each test. This is the type of test that requires ample preparation and practice if valid results are to be obtained. "Its administration is best learned under the direction of a person who has had experience in the analysis and correction of reading difficulties" (Durrell & Catterson, 1980, p. 12). The authors consider the observation of difficulties the most important factor in the DARD; consequently, the check lists are extremely important. Also important is a sound knowledge of each test so the examiner can quickly decide if the administration of other subtests will contribute helpful information to understanding a student's difficulties.

Technical Aspects

Revisions of the DARD were based on three major sources of data. The first source included critical reviews, evaluations in textbooks, research articles, clinical reports, competing instruments, the authors' research, and correspondence from users of the DARD.

The second source of information was the response from 200 of 250 professors who used the DARD in their reading courses. These professors responded to tentative proposals to change. Based on the responses, "the most urgent needs were new normative data, updating and modifying paragraph content, checking placement, and clearing up confusion about certain tests" (Durrell & Catterson, 1980, p. 7). The authors also noted that "proposals for devoting more space to test rationale and remedial suggestions were generally rejected" (Durrell & Catterson, 1980, p. 7).

A third source of information was tryouts of the revised edition with approximately 200 students per grade in each of grades one through six who had average stanine scores on the Metropolitan Reading Test. The tryouts were conducted in five regions of the United States near universities with strong graduate programs in reading. Local university staff assisted in identifying the communities to be involved in the standardization. After the DARD was administered, these data were analyzed to obtain norms. A separate analysis for each of the states involved in the standardization showed close agreement in each grade from region to region. No detailed data from these tryouts are presented in the manual.

☐ Validity

The bulk of the validity for the DARD is historical in that the content of the DARD has remained relatively stable from revision to revision. This fact, according to the authors, "attests to current professional confidence in its general validity" (Durrell & Catterson, 1980, p. 57).

Content validity for the passages in the Oral Reading, Silent Reading, and Listening Comprehension tests was strengthened by selecting content that was representative for the indicated level. In addition, the vocabulary words used in the passages were screened by standard word lists (not mentioned) and refined through field testing.

Predictive validity was determined for several prereading tests administered in September and used to predict June reading achievement. The correlations were about .65 for Syntax Matching, .60 for Writing Letters, .60 for Identifying Phonemes, and .55 for Naming Letters.

☐ Reliability

A number of tests were subjected to the application of the Kuder-Richardson Formula 21 with at least 200 students who took each test. The reliability coefficients ranged from .73 for the Phonic Spelling and Visual Memory of Words (Intermediate) tests to .97 for the Spelling (Intermediate) test. The Word Recognition and Word Analysis tests had reliability coefficients ranging from .81 at the primary level (25 items) to .91 when 75 items were used.

Correlations were also reported among selected DARD tests for the primary and intermediate grades. Among the tests for the primary grades, the lowest correlation was between Listening Vocabulary and Listening Comprehension (.22). Apparently these two listening tests are not measuring the same trait. The highest correlation was .94 between Word Recognition and Word Analysis.

Among the tests in the intermediate grades, the lowest correlation was between Spelling and Silent Reading (.42). The highest correlation was .96 between Word Recognition and Word Analysis, almost identical with that found in similar tests for the primary grades.

Correlations were calculated between DARD tests and grade equivalent scores of the Metropolitan Reading Tests. Resulting correlations were at or above .85 for the Oral Reading tests and Metropolitan grade equivalent scores.

Critique

The DARD is a series of tests for the individual assessment of a student's reading difficulties. The wide range of tests included in the analysis makes it suitable for the nonreader through students reading at the sixth grade level. Many professionals have apparently found the DARD useful, given its "increasing distribution" over the years (Durrell & Catterson, 1980, p. 7). Such professionals are probably in an excellent position to note both the strengths and limitations of the DARD. According to the authors, professionals identified four areas where improvements were needed: normative data, updating and modifying paragraph placement, checking placement, and clearing up confusion about certain tests.

□ Normative Data

The first area suggested for improvement was the need for new normative data. In this reviewer's opinion, the authors embarked on an ambitious standardization effort that had tremendous potential to provide in-depth data on validity, reliability, and norms. Unfortunately, the information presented in the Manual is much less than could have resulted. VanRoekel (1985) noted that "more adequate normative data could have been provided had the authors chosen to pay more attention to test theory" (p. 519). There is a better explanation of the basis for the new norms than in the previous edition; nevertheless, greater detail is still necessary for increased understanding and interpretation. For example, norms for the Oral Reading and Silent Reading tests are given in grade equivalents that are based on rate of reading (low, middle, and high) for each grade. There are no clear statements or statistical evidence showing how the criteria for low, middle, and high were determined. Such evidence would have provided a basis for evaluating both the significance and accuracy of these scores.

The validity of the DARD "is described in a most unsatisfactory way and is based largely on the test's longevity, the harvest of opinions from experts who use the test, and its stability of content over time" (Roser, 1985, p. 518). Perhaps the old adage, "if it ain't broke, don't fix it" characterizes the stance of the authors and publisher. Since the DARD has shown constantly increasing distribution, a revised edition should, in this reviewer's opinion, make a genuine effort to provide a reasonably complete statistical base for the various tests. The authors did propose devoting more space to test rationale, but the proposal was generally rejected (Durrell & Catterson, 1980). It would have been helpful to have such data presented so users could validate the authors' decisions. The information presented on reliability, however, is much stronger than that reported in the previous edition.

Because the basic nature of the test has remained constant over the years, the emphasis in the current edition is focused on specific skills and what could be called a deficit model of reading diagnosis. The authors might have devoted some attention to a student's strengths and how they could be incorporated into corrective or remedial programs.

□ Updating and Modifying Paragraph Content

The authors revised some passages slightly and prepared some completely new passages. These changes were the result of detailed study to update content, to avoid ethnic and sexual bias, and to achieve more curricular balance. A number of these changes appear to be primarily cosmetic (VanRoekel, 1985). In addition, Roser (1985) notes that in some cases, the detailed study was not very evident; moreover, the overall content was "dull" with a "mundane style" (p. 517) that could influence the student's performance.

Although the authors talk about equating the paragraphs in the Oral Reading, Silent Reading, and Listening Comprehension tests, no data are presented to support their claim. The results of readability analyses, syntactic complexity, and the like for each passage might have been presented in the Manual. It would have been helpful if they had shared their logic and evidence in their quest for equivalent paragraphs.

☐ Checking Placement

The DARD purports to help examiners establish the student's independent and instructional levels. Because the instructional level is often considered to be of primary importance, how it is determined with the DARD will be considered. An instructional level is assigned to the student if (1) the median grade on the time norms is achieved, and (2) the comprehension rating on that passage is at least fair. "Fair" comprehension varies from passage to passage, depending on the number of comprehension questions. For example, a rating of fair on passage 1B could be as low as 50 percent comprehension. For passage C, a minimum comprehension score of 66 percent is required. These comprehension scores are based on recall questions only, and the percentage criteria is lower than the 75 percent commonly cited by various reading authorities (Harris & Sipay, 1985; Hays, 1975). Explanations for the differing criteria and the use of only recall questions might have been presented in the Manual. The reading levels obtained through these procedures should be used with caution.

☐ Clearing up Confusion about Certain Tests

The authors fail to identify which tests require greater clarity; nevertheless, the Manual is more explicit and provides greater detail than the 1955 edition. This is a welcome change even though there are areas where additional detail and information would be helpful. For example, in the Oral Reading test, the examiner is told to disregard minor errors during oral reading, yet there are no specific guidelines for determining which errors are minor.

Roser (1985) questions the Identifying Letter Names in Spoken Words test because it presents a task "so alien to typical instruction that beginning readers are likely to experience confusion" (p. 517).

☐ Additional Comments

The Oral Reading tests require an examiner who is quick and careful in recording errors as a student reads. The authors' recommendation to tape record this test and any test in which the student makes an oral response is a good one. Recording hesitations is made more difficult because the number of words in each line of the passages in the student booklet do not consistently match the same lines in the Individual Record Booklet.

Professionals interested in the work of Goodman (1967) will note selected insights from miscue analysis although the term "miscue" is not used in the manual. Some errors (for example, repetitions and dialect) are not counted, and words miscalled but corrected are counted as half an error. If a student pauses on a word for five seconds, the examiner is directed to pronounce the word since time norms are a significant factor in determining reading levels. This practice deprives the examiner from noting the strategies the student uses to identify unknown words and may impact the student's comprehension of the passage.

Conclusions

If the four most urgent needs identified by the authors serve as the only basis for evaluating this revision of the DARD, the results are disappointing. The test's long history apparently won out over good test construction and more recent insights into the diagnosis of reading difficulties. The time and energy necessary to develop a diagnostic reading test based on a sound theory of reading and test construction may have been beyond the authors' desires and the publisher's commitment of financial resource.

All tests have limitations; therefore, the DARD must be evaluated within this context. The validity of the DARD is largely dependent on how users assess the test's content. The various tests of the DARD provide a means to assist professionals in assessing a student's reading. The range and variety of the tests and the flexibility in how the tests can be used are assets. Experienced examiners are urged to make modifications in the suggested administration procedures to maximize the student's performance.

The manual and reliability data for this revision of the DARD is improved. While some users might appreciate more miscue analysis strategies and suggestions for remediation, this edition of the DARD shows improvements. The standardization is much improved.

Those who have used earlier editions of the DARD will feel right at home. That comfort level may be one of the major reasons why the test will probably continue to enjoy widespread use. It remains to be seen whether the profession can make strides in the diagnosis of reading difficulties when the conceptual and psychometric properties of a widely used diagnostic test undergo so little change in 50 years.

References

Durrell, D. D., and Catterson, J. H. (1980). *Durrell Analysis of Reading Difficulty manual of directions*. New York: Psychological Corporation.

Harris, A. J., and Sipay, E. R. (1985). *How to increase reading ability* (8th ed.). New York: Longman.

Hays, W. S. (1975). *Criteria for the instructional level of reading.* (ERIC Document Reproduction Service No. ED 117 665)

Roser, N. L. (1985). Review of Durrell Analysis of Reading Difficulty, Third Edition. In J. V. Mitchell, Jr. (Ed.), *The ninth mental measurements yearbook*, Vol. 1, (pp. 516–18), Lincoln, NE: Buros Institute of Mental Measurements.

VanRoekel, B. H. (1985). Review of Durrell Analysis of Reading Difficulty, Third Edition. In J. V. Mitchell, Jr. (Ed.), *The ninth mental measurements yearbook*, Vol. 1, (pp. 518–19), Lincoln, NE: Buros Institute of Mental Measurements.

Gates-McKillop-Horowitz Reading Diagnostic Test

Authors: Arthur I. Gates, Ann S. McKillop, and Elizabeth C. Horowitz

Publisher: Teachers College Press

Edition: Second

Copyright: 1981

Reviewer: Robert B. Cooter, Jr., Bowling Green State University

General Description

The *Gates-McKillop-Horowitz Reading Diagnostic Test* is an individually administered array of tests intended for children in grades one through six. There are some 24 different scores possible in areas related to oral reading (12), word identification (2), decoding and letter identification (7), auditory discrimination and blending (2), and written expression (1). While the authors suggest that the purpose of the test is to identify "the strengths and weaknesses in reading and related areas of a particular child" (p. 3), the essence of reading, comprehension, has been omitted. Thus, the Gates-McKillop-Horowitz test may be viewed as an incomplete assessment instrument.

There are two booklets used in giving the tests, Test Materials and the Pupil Record Booklet. The Test Materials booklet serves as a set of stimulus materials to elicit student responses. These responses are recorded in the Pupil Record Booklet. A Manual of Directions booklet is also included to guide examiners through the diagnostic battery.

The 1981 revision of the Gates-McKillop-Horowitz test remains essentially the same as the original 1962 test, with two notable exceptions. First, the authors have included an optional informal writing sample stating that "the way a child approaches the writing task, is of diagnostic value." This seems to reflect the more holistic modes of literacy assessment of our time, a seemingly paradoxical twist for a test that views reading from a more fragmented perspective. Second, the 1981 revision addresses certain psychometric criticisms on reliability and norming noted for the earlier version of the Gates-McKillop test (Drum, 1985). Descriptions of the norming sample of 600 children in grades one through six are provided, along with data regarding oral reading subtest correlations, test-retest reliability on the oral reading subtest, and interjudge reliability. A discussion of these data is provided in the Technical Considerations portion of this review.

The authors state that the examiner should "learn to choose for each child only those tests that are necessary and thus to avoid wasting the time of both examiner and child" (Gates, McKillop, and Horowitz, 1981, p. 3). Hence, administration of the entire battery is not viewed as essential. A brief description of each test follows in the next section of this review.

Description of the Test Components

The first subtest, Oral Reading, is a series of seven paragraphs that tell a story about a dog and rat. Each paragraph is progressively more difficult, moving from presumably the first grade level through about the high sixth grade level. However, when one scrutinizes these paragraphs a little more closely using a modified Fry Graph for estimating readability, the first paragraph appears to be at about the second grade level, and the last paragraph at about the sixteenth grade level. Another criticism of these oral paragraphs is the use of archaic language (e.g., ...my noble rodent kinsman...; ...mayhap we shall permit thee the privilege of sojourning...) as a device for altering the readability level of the passages. This practice would seem to ignore the role of schematic structures and other prior learning in the application of word identification and recognition strategies. Clearly this was one aspect of the earlier Gates-McKillop test that should have been reworked for the present revision.

A positive feature of the Oral Reading subtest is the miscue analysis section. There are some nine error patterns noted on the front of the protocol for analysis purposes. These data could be used in conjunction with other assessment procedures to determine whether an actual error pattern exists related to word identification, fluency of reading, and perhaps, use of context.

While the listing of certain miscue patterns may be more or less consistent with some of the commercial informal reading inventories, there is an obvious weakness related to comprehension assessment. Specifically, there are no follow-up questions or retellings of the Oral Reading paragraphs. That may be just as well since the story offers very little in the way of plot or characterization. Another comprehension assessment problem has to do with the errors that are recorded. That is, when a child makes an error one might determine whether the miscue is graphically or grammatically similar, or if a meaning change has occurred (as with the *Reading Miscue Inventory*, Goodman, Watson, and Burke, 1987). While the miscue analysis section of the Oral Reading subtest is generally a positive concept, the lack of attention to reading comprehension must be viewed as a serious omission.

In addition to the Oral Reading, the authors have added a new Reading Sentences subtest. The stated purpose is to assess "the extent to which the child uses meaning clues or word-form clues in word recognition" (p. 6). A rationale for including these four sentences on the 1981 revision is not offered for this seemingly superfluous subtest.

The next two subtests pertain to word identification and are very similar in format to the subtest on the Durrell Analysis of Reading Difficulty. The examiner is provided with a tachistoscope with which to flash a series of sight words of untimed analysis. The intention for each subtest is to evaluate the child's ability to identify words without the aid of context clues. The selection criteria for the 40 words included on each subtest is not explained in the manual, thus making it difficult to determine the efficacy of the subtests themselves.

Word Attack is the next major portion of the test. This series of subtests utilizes exclusively nonsense words to measure such reading skills as syllabication, recognizing and blending word parts, and reading unknown words. The remainder of the section has to do with giving letter sounds and alphabet recognition. The manual suggests that this subtest helps examiners evaluate decoding and encoding skills, albeit in a fragmentary way. One problem with this splintered perspective for assessing reading skills is that children who have not been exposed to synthetic phonics instruction may do poorly on this subtest even though they may be quite fluent readers.

Auditory Discrimination is a test included on the 1981 edition which measures the student's ability to differentiate between speech sounds in phonetically similar words. This skill is thought to be closely linked to the child's ability to acquire phonics skills.

A new addition to the Gates-McKillop-Horowitz test is the Auditory Blending section. On this subtest the child listens to the examiner pronounce a word slowly in syllables, then he or she must blend and repeat the word as it would normally sound. Again, a clear rationale for inclusion of this subtest was not offered in the manual, and according to the authors, all children in the norm group seemed to perform well. Thus, the diagnostic value of the Auditory Blending subtest is unclear.

The final test of the Gates-McKillop-Horowitz test is Written Expression which includes Spelling and optional Informal Writing Sample. Spelling is intended to assess the child's ability to spell isolated words that are both phonetically regular and irregular. The manual states that "important clues" for developing remedial plans may be derived from observing the child's methods of analyzing words in spelling (p. 15), but research does not seem to support this assumption. One other troubling aspect of the Spelling test is that the Manual fails to explain how these particular words were chosen.

A new addition to the 1981 revision is the optional Informal Writing Sample. As mentioned previously, this seems to reflect the resurgent interest in holistic assessment and teaching of our time. On this subtest the child is asked to write about any topic of interest according to their ability. It is noted in the Manual that some children may only write one sentence while others may produce much more sophisticated compositions. Criteria are offered for evaluating the composition, but no norms are included for this informal exercise. While this subtest does not seem to be fully developed, it offers the examiner a much more viable perspective for assessing the child's literacy behaviors. However, until this test is more fully developed and includes research-supported means for interpretation it should be omitted.

Technical Aspects

Major criticisms of the 1962 version of the Gates-McKillop test were that no description of the norm group was offered, and data on reliability and validity were not offered (Gable, 1981). These complaints were addressed to some extent in the 1981 revision by including rather specific demographic information about the 600 children who participated in the field testing. These children attended ten different schools (65 percent private schools, 83 percent urban), were from various racial/ethnic communities (64 percent caucasian, 37 percent black, 4 percent oriental), and all were English speaking, (14 percent speak Spanish in the home). The field testing was completed in the spring and fall of 1979 and the spring of 1980 (p. 3). Descriptions of the norm group did not include socioeconomic information, nor was it indicated how the children were selected.

Test-retest reliability is reported to be .94 on the Oral Reading test and concurrent validity indices range from a low of .68 in the upper grades to a high of .96 in the lower grades. The interrated (referred to as "interjudge" in the manual) reliability ratings for error classifications range from 94 percent agreement for the easier paragraphs to 91 percent agreement on the more difficult paragraphs. Although the empirical characteristics of the Oral Reading test seem to be acceptable, the validity of using limited context and seemingly archaic language is questionable.

The technical data on test reliability and validity described in the manual deal exclusively with the Oral Reading test. However, norms tables for the Words: Flash, Words: Untimed, and the Spelling test are provided without empirical support or explanation.

In summary, the reliability estimates reported seem to be quite adequate for the Oral Reading test, but are not reported for the other tests. Likewise, standard error of measurement data are not reported. The validity of the Oral Reading test seems questionable. The demographic data provided should help examiners to determine whether the norms provided are relevant to the child they are to test.

Conclusions

The strength of the Gates-McKillop-Horowitz Reading Diagnostic Tests is its revised Manual of Directions. It is clear, concise, and quite readable. The Manual provides a technical data section not included in the earlier edition and offers directions for administering each test in a most comprehensible format.

A major weakness of the Reading Diagnostic Tests is the exclusion of comprehension measures. According to Farr (1986), reading is comprehension. To construct an assessment instrument devoid of comprehension measurements is to create an insurmountable validity problem.

Other weaknesses of the Reading Diagnostic Tests are incomplete normative data, an Oral Reading Test that utilizes archaic languages and passages with extremely high readability levels, and a philosophical approach to reading diagnosis based on essentialism rather than a holistic perspective. Hence, one must conclude that this test has rather limited utility.

The Reading Diagnostic Tests should be viewed as an instrument to be used only by those who are willing to supplement the information it can provide with much informal diagnosis concerning how students actually use and monitor the strategies they bring to the printed page (Pearson and Herman, 1985, pp. 602–03). In this way the examiner will be able to investigate most of the crucial aspects of the reading act and verify patterns of weakness.

References

Drum, P. A. (1985). Review of Gates-McKillop-Horowitz Reading Diagnostic Test, Second Edition. In J. V. Mitchell (Ed.), *The ninth mental measurements yearbook*. Lincoln, NE: The University of Nebraska Press.

Farr, R., and Carey, R. F. (1986). *Reading: What can be measured?* (2nd ed.). Newark, DE: International Reading Association.

Gable, S. (1981). Test review: Gates-McKillop Reading Diagnostic Tests. In L. M. Schell (Ed.), *Diagnostic and criterion referenced reading tests: Review and evaluation.* Newark, DE: International Reading Association.

Gates, A. I.; McKillop, A. S.; and Horowitz, E. C. (1981). Gates-McKillop-Horowitz Reading Diagnostic Test (2nd ed.). New York: Teachers College Press.

Goodman, Y.; Watson, D. J.; and Burke, C. L. (1987). *Reading miscue inventory: Alternative procedures.* New York: Richard C. Owen.

Pearson, P. D., and Herman, P. (1985). Review of Gates-McKillop-Horowitz Reading Diagnostic Test, Second Edition. In J. V. Mitchell (Ed.), *The ninth mental measurements yearbook*. Lincoln, NE: The University of Nebraska Press.

Woodcock Reading Mastery Tests–Revised

Authors: Richard W. Woodcock, Nancy Mather, and Elaine K. Barnes

Publisher: American Guidance Service

Edition: Second

Range: Kindergarten to Adult

Copyright: 1987

Reviewer: Don A. Brown, Educational Diagnostics, Englewood, Colorado

General Description

The *Woodcock Reading Mastery Tests–Revised* (WRMT–R) is a revision of the original 1973 version. It retains the same general format and tests as the earlier edition but introduces a Visual-Auditory Learning test, an enlarged Word Comprehension test, the inclusion of norms for college and adults, and changes in the Summary of Scores and interpretation. It is available in Form G with the complete test battery, and Form H which does not include the readiness tests and Supplementary Letter Checklist. A Record Form G+H is also available for use in combining the two separate forms. The WRMT–R no longer uses the term "Relative Mastery Score" as in the 1973 edition, renaming this interpretive score the "Relative Performance Index."

The WRMT–R is a durable and well-designed battery of six individually administered tests intended to measure reading skills and abilities from kindergarten through adulthood. Its design reveals a traditional philosophy of reading, dividing measurement into three "clusters": Readiness, Basic Skills, and Reading Comprehension.

Reading Readiness is measured through tests of Visual-Auditory Learning and Letter Identification; Basic Skills are measured through tests of Word Identification and Word Attack; and Reading Comprehension is measured through the tests of Word Comprehension and Passage Comprehension. The Word Comprehension test includes the subtests of Antonyms, Synonyms, and Analogies. A Total Reading Score-Full Scale is obtained by combining scores on Word Identification, Word Attack, Word Comprehension, and Passage Comprehension.

A Total Reading-Short Scale provides a faster estimate by using only Word Identification and Passage Comprehension.

The Visual-Auditory Learning test, taken from the *Woodcock-Johnson Psycho-Educational Battery* uses rebuses in tasks simulating learning to read. Although norms are given through college, mean scores do not increase significantly above third grade level. The mean raw score for third graders is listed as 115 correct responses compared to 50 year old adults with 116 correct.

The Letter Identification test measures ability to identify letters by name or by sound. Difficulty at higher levels is introduced through the use of unusual type styles, although again there is no significant increase in mean scores reported above third grade level. Visual-Auditory Learning and Letter Identification scores are combined to provide an estimate of reading readiness. It seems unfortunate that such a carefully prepared battery has not included a broader and more trustworthy measure of reading readiness. The two readiness tests are not computed in the total reading score, an improvement over the 1973 edition in which letter identification was included as part of total reading. A Supplementary Letter Checklist printed in sans serif type face is added as a check list for capital and lower case letter identification, but not included in the norms nor in computing either readiness or total reading.

The Word Identification test presents 106 words in isolation, scaling the test from kindergarten through college to adulthood. Difficulty at the upper levels is produced through obscurity of words which are admittedly "difficult even for above average college students" (WRMT–R *Test Book*). The subject is simply asked to name the word—comprehension is not implied. There is no differentiation between those who identify words through automatic recognition and those who identify them through word analysis.

The Word Attack test requires subjects to pronounce nonsense words, correctness of their pronunciation based on the application of common phonic and structural analysis principles. As with most tests using nonsense words, problems exist in the form of awkward word structures ("translibsodge" seems unusually difficult to pronounce) and the clash between the legitimate method of analysis and another ("vauge" is to be pronounced "vawj," although a reader familiar with the word "gauge" might legitimately choose initial consonant substitution, pronouncing the word "vayj"). Although the norms would indicate placement at elementary, secondary, college, and adult levels, the tasks included are not generally recognized as a part of reading development nor of common instructional content above the middle elementary level. No mention is made of sources used in the construction of this portion of the test, and no data are presented to substantiate a systematic inclusion of word analysis elements. Some graphemes have little applicability, particularly at the upper levels where unusual forms appear to be used to create artificial difficulty, as in the nonsense words "cigbet," "bafmotbem," "monglustamer," or "translibsodge," which bear little resemblance to common English word forms. The use of nonsense words removes the "leap to recognition" possible when actual words are used. With nonsense words, the subject has no chance of recognizing the word, and, there-fore, cannot use eventual recognition as an aid to word attack. Older subjects who tend to use recognizability as an aid to analysis are at an even greater disadvantage than younger subjects who are more often content to produce a wordlike sound without regard for recognizing the word. Once again, although norms are provided through college, there is little discrimination above third grade: a raw score of 28 yields a grade equivalent score of 3.7; 32 yields 5.9; and 36 yields 13.1. Raw scores 37 through 45 all yield a grade equivalent of 16.9. Word Identification and Word Attack are combined to indicate the subject's basic skills level.

A significant improvement over the original edition is the classification sys-tem which has been built into the Word Attack test to help identify the subject's skill deficits. The test administrator can identify the part of each word that has caused the reader difficulty, developing a profile of word attack skills. It seems unfortunate that a test of this sort which appears destined for wide usage has no assessment of the subject's ability to use context clues or the syntax of the sentence in identifying unfamiliar words.

The Word Comprehension test includes three subtests: Antonyms, Synonyms, and Analogies. In the Antonyms subtest the subject reads each word as it is presented and then supplies a word with the opposite meaning. In the Synonyms subtest, the subject reads each word and then gives a word with approximately the same meaning. On the Analogies subtest the subject reads three related words and supplies a fourth word, completing the relationship.

In Analogies, the 79 words are divided into general, science and math, social studies, and humanities vocabularies. By combining both forms G and H, a larger pool of words in each area can be obtained and a better evaluation made, but without that, the limited number of words is hardly large enough to give a satisfactory picture of vocabulary adequacy in the four areas. Also, since subjects must read the first three words for themselves before solving the analogy, it is presumable that some of the errors are caused because they cannot correctly identify those three words rather than because they do not know the correct word to supply at the end of the analogy. Nevertheless, the range from kinder-garten through college to adulthood would seem more logically justified on Word Comprehension than either the Basic Skills Cluster or the Readiness Cluster.

The Passage Comprehension test utilizes a modified cloze technique ranging from a phrase or sentence with an accompanying picture of the easier levels, to a short two-sentence passage as it becomes more difficult. The subjects read the materials to themselves and supply answers in the form of a one-word fill-in response. There would appear to be more comprehension measures of under-standing than predicting a missing word. There is not an attempt to assess the higher levels of reading such as reading appreciation, critical reading, evaluation, or inferential reading. This test is not immune to the problems of other reading tests in confusion between word recognition and reading comprehension. Subjects who have significant difficulty with word recognition do poorly on the Passage Comprehension test, but their difficulty will be reported not as one of poor word recognition, but as a problem with comprehension.

In addition, some subjects appear to make good use of the picture clues the authors have included at the lower levels of the test, having greater difficulty with passages without picture clues. This leads to the question of whether earlier good performance was due to good reading ability or the ability to gain meaning from the pictures included with the material. Finally, although the test is advertised as useable for secondary, college, and adults subjects, the choice of vocabulary in this section tends to be childish, in contrast to the vocabularies in the Word Comprehension tests which appear to be inoffensive to adults.

The plates used to administer the tests are supported in a sturdy ring binder that props up between the examiner and the subject so that on one side the subject sees the test item while on the other side the examiner sees the item reprinted with additional directions for administration.

The Examiner's Manual tends to be complete in its coverage but somewhat cumbersome in its use. Although its format and appearance are impressive, its size is forbidding. Significant space is devoted to such topics as general test administration, qualifications of test administrators, practice exercises, partial duplication of test descriptions in chapters one and two, case studies, and a section on the confidentiality of test results. Such materials balloon the manual and hide more useful information. An index would help the examiner find needed topics more quickly.

Supplementary materials include a cassette tape to standardize pronunciation of words in the tests, a Report to Parents form, and an optional microcomputer scoring program disk.

Different kinds of interpretations are possible with the WRMT–R: some sections lend themselves to use as criterion-referenced tests without using the norms at all. The Summary of Scores included in the Test Record form guides the examiner through the scoring process from raw scores to various derived scores such as grade equivalent scores, "age scores," percentile ranks, and standard scores. The Relative Performance Index is an additional interpretation, yielding a ratio indicative of the quality of performance on a test. In addition, Instructional Ranges are indicated, presumably "directly parallel to the difference between the *independent* and *frustration* reading levels of the informal reading inventory (IRI) procedure described by Betts (1957)." The *Examiner's Manual* continues, "The WRMT–R instructional range also has the added benefits of standardized presentation and more precise (reliable) measurement" (p. 40).

It seems the authors hoped to provide a measure that would indicate subjects' IRI functional reading levels by using Word Identification (isolated word recognition), Word Attack, Word Comprehension (antonyms, synonyms, and analogies), and Passage Comprehension tests (modified cloze procedure). No research is cited to back that expectation, and unfortunately the various kinds of tests listed above have not tended to give a very reliable indication of IRI functional reading levels.

Technical Aspects

In general, the report on the technical procedures of the WRMT–R is one of the strongest features of this publication. Data on reliability and validity are clearly presented and easily available. The norms for the test are clearly presented and appear to be technically accurate.

☐ Reliability

The technical data supplied with the WRMT–R are generally satisfactory with median split-half reliabilities ranging from .84 to .98. As might be expected from earlier comments in this evaluation, the Letter Identification Test proves less reliable, with the reliabilities reported from as high as .94 at grade one to as low as .34 at grade level five. Split-half reliabilities for the Readiness Cluster (Visual-Auditory and Letter Identification) are high at first grade with .97, but, as would be expected, become low, .54, at fifth grade. Test–retest reliabilities are not reported, although in the original 1973 version they were reported and were found to follow a somewhat similar pattern to that reported with split-half reliabilities, showing good reliability for four of the subtests, but with Letter Identification dropping from .84 at grade level 2.9 to .16 at the 7.9 grade level.

☐ Validity

Content Validity. In predicting reading readiness, the WRMT–R uses the Visual-Auditory Learning test rather than measures of visual discrimination of letters, auditory discrimination of phonemes and words, adequacy of language base, or other variables having a more closely established relationship with initial reading readiness. For Word Attack and Word Identification, there is no direct measure of the subject's ability to use the context as an aid in either word identification or word analysis, although it is widely recognized as a critical ingredient in both skills.

In Reading Comprehension, there are no measures of comprehension skills other than those yielded through one-word replies to test items requiring little reading. Seventy-seven items required reading one word, 79 require reading three words, and another 79 require reading two sentences, at most. In addition, there are no measures of locational skills, reading study skills, fluency, or reading rate. For a publication that will receive major use in reading assessment, these are serious deficiencies.

Concurrent Validity. Concurrent validity figures reported compare the WRMT (1973) with the *Iowa Test of Basic Skills* and the *Iowa Tests of Educational Development*. On samples of 76 for third grade, 78 for fifth, and 40 for twelfth, correlations are .83, .78, and .79, respectively.

Norms. The extension of the norms through college to adulthood is a noble effort, but it has fallen heir to the problems others have encountered trying to do the same thing, basically, that there is not a linear relationship in reading development from elementary school through college into adulthood. To try to impose such a relationship by judging college seniors or adults on child-based measures of reading readiness or word analysis skills demonstrates a lack of understanding of the development of mature reading skills. The same is true when expecting meaningful scores by kindergarteners or first graders on analogies, antonyms, or synonyms developed to measure reading skills of older subjects.

In addition, to assume adulthood to be on a continuum beyond college misunderstands the relationship between college and later years. College seniors tend to be a select group of capable adult readers. When the norms are extended beyond college seniors to an adult sample including those with no formal education as well as those who are college graduates, the norms become less than useful. There is a great demand from those working with reading at secondary, community college, and adult levels for the sort of thing the authors have done, but the fact of the matter is that it is misleading to use a child-based instrument and simply extend its norms to secondary, college, and adult subjects. It is more than a reading truism that adults, whether college students or those in adult literacy programs, are not just tall first graders.

Conclusions

Although the WRMT–R is an impressive-appearing individually administered measure of reading abilities, its performance falls somewhat short of its promise. The statistical work on the test is above average, but fails to compensate for the fact that performance on the test tends to be weighted toward letter discrimination and other more mechanical aspects of reading with less effort placed on the measurement of the meaning side of reading. An administrator must weigh the disadvantage of individual administration against the rather meager gain realized from the individual attention rendered.

□ Advantages

The advantages of this test include sturdy construction, clear directions, ease of use in administration, good reliability, and numerous norms for use in test interpretation. It has a complete user's manual, an appealing format, two forms, a new short form for faster estimation of reading level, and a new error classification system built into the word attack section. Undoubtedly it is one of the most attractive reading tests on the market.

☐ Disadvantages

The WRMT–R does not include measures of context clues or use of syntax, locational skills, reading study skills, reading comprehension, fluency, or rate. It does not adequately measure reading comprehension or functional reading levels even though it is an individually administered test. The WRMT–R tends to be weaker than might be hoped for in the measurement of initial reading readiness. It depends on item obscurity for difficulty at the upper levels, and makes use of nonsense words—some peculiarily structured—to test word analysis skills. The college and adult norms are inadequate. Although the examiner's manual is complete, it is cumbersome to use.

References

Woodcock, R. W. (1987). *Woodcock Reading Mastery Test–Revised.* Circle Pines, MN: American Guidance Service, Inc.

Woodcock, R. W. (1987). *Woodcock Reading Mastery Tests–Revised examiner's manual.* Circles Pines, MN: American Guidance Service, Inc.

Woodcock, R. W. (1973). *Woodcock Reading Mastery Tests.* Circle Pines, MN: American Guidance Service, Inc.

Woodcock, R. W. (1973). *Woodcock Reading Mastery Tests, manual.* Circle Pines, MN: American Guidance Service, Inc.

GROUP READING TESTS

Introduction

There are times when it becomes necessary for teachers, administrators, and reading researchers to determine the reading ability of more than one student in a single sitting. Group reading tests make this possible. Three group administered reading tests have been selected for review reflecting choices available in this genre. While they may vary somewhat in content many similarities exist. First, group reading tests tend to be norm-referenced. This feature is very appealing for school administrators requiring some sort of documentation of curricular success. Second, these tests are usually available in different forms for pre- and posttest measurements. Thus, these tests are not only attractive to school systems, but also to researchers interested in quantitative analyses. A third feature of group reading tests is that they usually have several levels available, matching learners at different grade levels (e.g., the new Gates-MacGinitie Reading Tests, 3rd edition, has levels available from level PRE for kindergarten children through level 10/12 for high school students) with a test of appropriate difficulty.

Some of the questions one should consider when selecting a group reading test follow:

1. Is there a good match between the reading abilities being measured and those taught in the reading classroom (content/curricular validity)?
2. Are the philosophy of reading used by the test makers and the philosophy used in the reading classroom compatible (construct validity)?
3. Are the reliability norms acceptable?
4. Do the test publishers provide alternatives for scoring the test booklets, such as machine or hand scoring?
5. Are the time limits allowed for completion of subtests appropriate at each level in terms of maturity expectations?
6. Do the examples clearly define the tasks to be completed?
7. Are the directions for administering and scoring clear and complete?

Gates-MacGinitie Reading Tests, Third Edition

Authors: Walter H. MacGinitie and Ruth K. MacGinitie

Publisher: The Riverside Publishing Company

Edition: Third

Copyright: 1989

Reviewers: Robert L. Aaron, University of Georgia
Cindy Gillespie, Ball State University

General Description

The Gates-MacGinitie Reading Tests, Third Edition, are group administered measures of reading readiness skills and language concepts, the beginning reading skills at grade one, and, at grades two through twelve, vocabulary and comprehension mastery. The tests are designed primarily for evaluating student reading progress but may be used as a way to assess groups within classes and to compare classes, schools, and school systems. They are also useful in reporting to parents.

The Pre-Reading Test evaluates language skills, letter knowledge, and ability to discriminate sounds auditorially. The R-level test, grade 1.0 through 1.9, evaluates phonics skills knowledge and skill at use of context clues. Both tests, in addition to supplying normative data, may be interpreted diagnostically. The Level One test may be used to evaluate students who come into a first grade between five and nine months into the school year having mastered the mechanics of the basic phonics and context clue skills and who need to be evaluated for vocabulary and comprehension skill mastery. Beginning with the Level One test, and continuing through Level 10/12 (grades 1.5 through 12.9), the tests measure Vocabulary and Comprehension mastery.

The test format is multiple choice, allowing for group testing, and provides machine and hand scorable booklets for Levels PRE through 3. At grades four through twelve machine scored and self scoring answer sheets are available. The Prereading, Readiness, and Level One (kindergarten through 1.9) tests have one form while Levels Two through 10/12 (2.0 through 12.9) have two forms each.

The new Gates-MacGinitie Tests contain normative tables and directions for use of out-of-level norms, and for out-of-level testing. Normative tables are available for fall, winter, and spring testing dates and directions are included for computing an interpolation ratio for use in adjusting the norms to a date other than the three (fall, winter, spring) on which the tests may have been given. At Levels One and Two (1.5-1.9, and 2.0-2.9), and Four through 10/12, (4.0 through 12.9) a classroom of pupils may be administered two different level tests, at the same time because the practice exercises and time factors are the same for these levels. Below Level One, separate testings must be carried out for classes in which pupils need an easier test in order to achieve a valid score, because parts of the test must be presented orally. Separate, grade-appropriate normative tables are available for students in the same chronological grade level taking different grade level tests. The teacher's manual contains a chart of test levels and directions on how to use the out-of-level norms and how to select pupils for out-of-level testing. Also discussed are use of the test by Title I examiners, and minority and Title IX considerations. There is also a discussion of prerequisite skills needed by young students prior to testing, as well as information on timing, pacing, and testing materials needed.

A significant addition to the third edition is an extensive section on using the test results in planning instruction.

□ Description of Subtests

Level PRE (Prereading Evaluation) has subtests for (1) Literacy Concepts, (2) Reading Instruction Relational Concepts, (3) Oral Language Concepts, and (4) Letters and Letter-Sound Correspondences. All subtests are preceded by a thorough practice period during which pupils are taught the prerequisite test-taking skills.

The Level PRE test measures background concepts that are important for learning to read.

The Literacy Concepts subtest measures knowledge of concepts such as "letter," "word," and "beginning of a book."

The Reading Instruction Relational Concepts subtest evaluates pupil knowledge of such ideas as "last," "middle," "same," "before," and "after."

The Oral Language Concepts subtest assesses the pupil's ability to select the picture name which begins with the same sound as the stimulus picture name. In addition to initial sound matching, there is some evaluation of final sound discrimination, and of word sound length.

Letters and Letter-Sound Correspondences is a test of the ability to visually match lower and upper-case letters singly, and in clusters resembling words. Also, there are test items which require the pupils to match a letter to a picture by thinking letter or sound correspondence, and, after saying the three picture names, select the matching initial letter or sound.

The Level R test (1.0 to 1.9) measures beginning reading skills in four skill areas (1) initial consonants and consonant clusters, (2) final consonants and consonant clusters, (3) vowels, and (4) use of context clues.

The three tests of consonant knowledge evaluate pupil knowledge using both picture/word and letter/picture items. Context clue use ability is assessed using brief sentences with word blanks which must be completed by selecting the proper word from four possible choices. The sentences and word answer choices are composed from sight vocabulary which normally is taught at the first grade level.

Beginning at Level One and continuing through Level 10/12 (1.0 to 12.9), all the tests contain subtests of Vocabulary and Comprehension. Levels One and Two measure vocabulary knowledge using a stimulus picture and four word choices. The Comprehension subtests in Levels One and Two present concepts in one, two, and three sentence paragraphs which are to be read and comprehension indicated through selection of a picture answer. In the Levels Three through 10/12 Vocabulary subtests, the target words appear in sentence context and are responded to by selection of the correct synonym. Comprehension is tested by use of reading paragraphs that evaluate both literal and critical thinking skill using a multiple choice response format.

Technical Aspects

Normative scores for the third edition of the Gates-MacGinitie tests were developed in 1987 to 1988. A sampling plan based on geographic region, enrollment size, family income, adults' years of schooling, parochial school attendance, sex, and ethnic composition was used. Methods of marking answers, adequate time to complete items, the mechanics of marking in booklets versus answer sheets, and training of pupils in prerequisite test-taking skills were evaluated and adjusted so they would not be significant factors in any differences in test scores.

Reliability coefficients for the Gates-MacGinitie Level One through Level 10/12 test are adequately high for both the Vocabulary and Comprehension subtests.

Test validity was established for the Vocabulary subtest by selecting words that are characteristic of the words read and mastered by students in grades one through twelve. For Levels PRE and R and Vocabulary test words for Levels One through 10/12, word lists from the Harris-Jacobson "Core Words and the Living Word Vocabulary" list were used to guide the selection of vocabulary test items. A balance of nouns, verbs, adjectives, and other speech parts was achieved from the first grade through twelfth grade. The Dale "List of 3000 Words Known by Students in Grade Four" and Francis and Kucera's *Frequency Analysis of English Usage: Lexicon and Grammar* were used to get this balance.

The Comprehension test subject-matter emphasizes fictional story material at the early grades, with emphasis on using material from poetry, natural sciences, social sciences, the arts, and fiction passages at the upper grades. Stories for the Level One and Two tests, which are for grades one and two, were written to achieve a high level of interest and to maintain a sentence pattern structure and readability in keeping with what pupils normally read in school at this age. Meyer's *Classification of Semantic Structures* was used in their development. Levels Three through 10/12 tests readings were drawn from published stories. Although they are power tests, sufficient time is allotted so that all but the very slowest students will finish the tests. Items which were poorly written or offensive to minority students were eliminated or rewritten. Readability of the passages was evaluated using the Dale-Chall, Fry, and Harris-Jacobson formulas.

Detailed worksheets and directions are included to aid scoring of the tests and to guide in interpolating scores from tests which may have been administered on dates other than those dates given for the fall, winter, and spring norms. Guidance is also given for adjusting the scores if the school opening date is different from that of the date used in the norming sample. There is a thorough treatment of test scoring, eliminating invalid tests, and using the norm tables. Types of test scores given are Percentile Ranks, Normal Curve Equivalents, and Stanines for judging a pupil's progress and standing relative to other students. Extended scale scores allow the progress of a student to be evaluated over a number of years using the same continuous scale. Grade equivalents are included with an extensive discussion of their proper uses, including cautions about a literal interpretation of a score as meaning the pupil can read, and has mastered the skills, on that grade level.

Conclusions

The Gates-MacGinitie Reading Tests evaluate prereading, readiness, vocabulary, and comprehension skill mastery from grades kindergarten through twelve. Supplementary out-of-level normative tables, and identical practice exercises and similar time limits make it possible for the examiner to test in the same room and evaluate pupils whose grade levels are different by using forms appropriate for them. Level PRE and R tests (grades kindergarten through 1.9) can be analyzed for language, letter, visual or auditory discrimination, phonics, and context clue use skills. Vocabulary is tested from grades 1.5 through 12.9 using the Levels One through 10/12 tests. The test items contain wrong answers that look like the word by initial, medial, or final position, or some combination of two of these three. Also, other possible answers are words that are "associated in meaning with the target word, but are not a synonym for it." The Vocabulary subtest contains words identified by all the major word lists as appropriate for all or some students on the grade level at which they are placed.

A combination of literal and inferential comprehension questions appropriate to the grade level is used beginning at Level One with literal and inferential questions and there is a systematic increase in the number of inference questions through Level 10/12. The tests include questions on the major skills of main idea, inferring character traits, inferencing about author's style, cause and effect, and sequence. Although a skill breakdown is not included, the examiner may get some diagnostic data by using the section on "Using the Scores in Instruction" in which there are discussions such as how to determine from wrong answers if a student is relying on prior knowledge, rather than reading accurately, for an answer.

The test is excellent for establishing the pupil's standardized reading score which may be needed to determine if the student qualifies for exceptional children services.

Also, it allows the "screening-out" of pupils who may need additional reading deficit diagnosis using more individualized and/or criterion testing.

The extensive normative tables and thorough, readable directions for their use, and a detailed section on interpolating local test scores from the tables, are excellent. Also included is a good discussion of the various test scores that may be administered and their proper uses.

The tests from PRE through Level 10/12, contain an excellent discussion of how to use the scores in the instructional program. There are General Strategies for Teaching the prereading, readiness, vocabulary and comprehension skills and this section contains many subclassifications of skill deficiencies. It discusses how to evaluate performance on the Gates-MacGinitie Tests, and sometimes suggests additional individual testing techniques which may be used to help arrive at a clearer statement of a pupil's exact skill needs. The subclassifications of reading problems contain suggestions about "good reading practices" and a strong listing of remedial procedures. A good feature of this section is the inclusion of several reference sources for each set of recommendations.

In the context of its purpose—a group standardized test of important preschool and beginning reading skills, vocabulary, and comprehension—the testing program is well conceived. From the standpoint of the reading diagnostician it contains good samples of these preschool and beginning reading skills, and appropriate vocabulary and comprehension skills pupils are called on to master in their reading program. The tests are an excellent first screening for large groups of students and can also be used to identify pupils at the beginning reading stage who need additional specific skill evaluation. The discussion of evaluation procedures and recommendations for remediation are excellent and are a strong feature of the testing program.

Metropolitan Achievement Test— MAT6 Reading Diagnostic Tests

Authors: Roger Farr, George Prescott, Irving Balow, and Thomas Logan

Publisher: The Psychological Corporation

Edition: Sixth

Copyright: 1986

Reviewer: George Canney, University of Idaho

General Description

The *Reading Diagnostic Tests* (RDT) is part of an integrated set of diagnostic and survey batteries titled MAT6. The complete series includes the Metropolitan Achievement Tests (1984), Metropolitan Language Diagnostic Test (1986), Metropolitan Mathematics Diagnostic Test (1986), Metropolitan Writing Test (1986) and the Reading Diagnostic Tests (1986). The RDT employs a multiple choice, paper and pencil format to provide information on reading strengths and weaknesses in eleven skill areas. The typical test item offers three or four choices, from which the student selects an answer by blackening in the appropriate circle using a #2 pencil.

There are six levels in this battery spanning grades K.5 through 9.9, with two Forms (L, M) for each level (the Primer level uses only Form L). Each level contains six or seven tests, except for the Advanced level (7.0 through 9.9) which has four tests. As shown in Table 3, lower levels of the RDT emphasize decoding skills such as letter recognition, sight vocabulary, and sound discrimination. Upper levels stress reading rate, skimming, and scanning, while vocabulary knowledge and comprehension are tested at all levels. It takes from about 1.5 to 2.5 hours and three to eight sittings to administer one level of the RDT. The lowest level can take a full week to give. (See Table 3.)

	Primer Grades K.5–1.9		Primary 1 Grades 1.5–2.9		Primary 2 Grades 2.5–3.9		Elementary Grades 3.5–4.9		Inter- mediate Grades 5.0–6.9		Advanced 1 Grades 7.0–9.9	
	Items	Min.	Items	Min.	Items	Min.	Items	Min.	Items	Min.	Items	Min.
Visual Discrimination	24	15										
Letter Recognition	26	15*										
Auditory Discrimination	24	25*	20	20*								
Sight Vocabulary	30	5*	30	5*	30	5*						
Phoneme/ Grapheme: Consonants	30	19*	27	20*	27	20*	24	20*	24	20*		

Table 3

Reading Diagnostic Tests Scope and Sequence Chart

* Test is dedicated or partially dedicated.

	Primer Grades K.5–1.9		Primary 1 Grades 1.5–2.9		Primary 2 Grades 2.5–3.9		Elementary Grades 3.5–4.9		Inter-mediate Grades 5.0–6.9		Advanced 1 Grades 7.0–9.9	
	Items	Min.	Items	Min.	Items	Min.	Items	Min.	Items	Min.	Items	Min.
Phoneme/ Grapheme: Vowels			30	17	36	20	42	25	42	25		
Vocabulary in Context	15	10	22	15	22	15	22	15	24	15	24	15
Word Part Clues			21	22	24	20	24	19	18	10		
Rate of Comprehension							33	5	35	4	31	4
Skimming and Scanning									20	20	20	20
Reading Comprehension	38	44	53	43	55	40	60	40	60	40	60	40
Total Diagnostic Battery	187	2 hrs. 13 min	203	2 hrs. 22 min	194	2 hrs.	205	2 hrs. 4 min.	223	2 hrs. 14 min.	135	1 hr. 19 min.

The Primer level (K.5 through 1.9) is the only level to test specifically for a student's ability to visually discriminate letters, letter clusters, and real and nonsense words. This level also tests for knowledge of upper and lower case letter names. The Auditory Discrimination test (Primer and Primary 1 levels) uses three-item multiple choice questions and pictures to check knowledge of initial and final consonant sounds. The examiner names each picture and reads the three words beneath. Students select the one word that starts, ends, or rhymes (Primary 1) with the same sounds as the name of the picture. Sight Vocabulary is tested at the first three levels by having students mark the word the examiner pronounces from a list of four words printed in the text booklet.

In The Phoneme/Grapheme Correspondence test consonants are tested in every level but the highest. Students pick the one word from three that begins or ends with the same sound(s) heard in the name of the picture read by the teacher. The teacher does not read the three answer choices. Knowledge of silent letter patterns is not tested until the Elementary and Intermediate levels. The

Phoneme/Grapheme Correspondence: Vowels (Primary 1 through Intermediate) differs from the test of consonant correspondences in that students are shown a target word with a vowel letter or letters underlined. Students must pronounce the target word without teacher assistance, then select the one word from a list of four that has the vowel sound heard in the target word. Often the spelling pattern in the target word is different from the spelling in the correct answer. The Word Part Clues test appears in levels Primary 1 through Intermediate. Students use sentence context clues to help them identify an omitted prefix, suffix or word within a compound word and indicate their choice by marking one of four words beneath each sentence.

Vocabulary in Context and Reading Comprehension are tested at all levels. A sentence completion format is used to check for vocabulary knowledge. At the Primer level, four types of items are used: match word to picture; match sentence with a rebus element to one of three pictures; match a picture to one of three sentences; and read short narrative selections and answer several questions. The Primary 1 level retains the rebus, sentence, and short passage formats; the remaining levels use only the passage and question format to measure reading comprehension. Text passages include a wide variety of genre and topics; test questions are, for the most part, text dependent, related to the focus questions provided prior to each test passage, and readable for the level intended.

Rate of Comprehension is assessed in the Elementary (3.5-4.9) to Advanced (7.0-9.9) levels using a modified cloze format. Each test has four passages of from 100 to 130 words that contain eight to ten deletions spaced at regular intervals and always at the ends of sentences. The vocabulary is at least one grade level below that for which the test was primarily developed. From three choices, students are to select the one word that fits the space. Scoring is based both on how many items a student answers and the number of items correct. Skimming and Scanning are assessed in the upper two levels of the RDT. Authentic texts reflecting the format of an encyclopedia are used to test the student's skill in locating specific details, making inferences, interpreting tables and graphs, and surveying material.

Examination kits for each level of the test are available at a modest price. It is strongly recommended that sets of 100 Practice Tests for each level be purchased and given to students a day or two before testing. These tests were used in the test development and norming stage of the RDT to familiarize students with the test format.

The RDT has features of both norm-referenced and criterion-referenced tests, so that it can be used to place students into a school reading program as well as to diagnose a student's reading skills. It can be administered by the regular classroom teacher without special training to larger groups as well as to one student at a time. Items within tests are grouped into clusters by objective so that performance on particular subskills, such as sequencing, short and long vowel sounds, prefixes and suffixes, and the like can be examined. The skill clusters highlighted on the RDT are also tested on the Survey Battery (general achievement) part of the MAT6. This permits the user to make comparisons between performance on the MAT6 Achievement Tests and the MAT6 Reading Diagnostic Tests. According to the authors, since scores on the RDT are statistically equated to scores in the same skill areas on the Achievement Tests, scores on the RDT can be treated both as norm-referenced and criterion-referenced indicators of reading performance. As norm-referenced data, raw scores are converted to percentile ranks, stanines, grade equivalents, scaled scores, and normal curve equivalents. The test also provides item p-values, proportion of students in a group reaching national norms, and figures about the average number of objectives passed. Criterion-referenced scores include: estimates of instructional, independent, and frustration reading levels; whether criteria for component skill objectives have or have not been reached; and performance categories describing Rate of Comprehension.

A wealth of support services and materials accompany the RDT; available at additional cost is a detailed manual for every level offering interpretive and prescriptive information and teaching suggestions for each test in the battery. The Manual for Interpreting includes explanations of the various types of test scores available with the RDT, sample student test profiles to study, and information on how the MAT6 was developed. A separate norms booklet is available for each level, though much of the information it contains is also in the Manual for Interpreting Tests. The norms booklet provides technical information on validity and reliability, plus numerous tables listing raw scores and conversion scores by test, by level, by time of year (fall and spring), and by grade. This information is valuable because it helps the test user interpret raw test scores in terms of instructional, independent, and frustration levels, as well as the significance of a student's test scores in light of his or her instructional reading level. In other words, the RDT norms booklet and the Manual for Interpreting contain tables that convert raw scores obtained on the reading comprehension test at each level into instructional, independent, and frustration reading levels. Another set of tables relates a student's performance on skill tests to his or her instructional reading level (IRL), and suggests that subskills covered in these tests are of *high*, *some*, or *low* importance for instruction. For example, the table suggests that when a student scores at a third grade reading level, visual discrimination and letter recognition are not of instructional concern: auditory discrimination, rate of comprehension, and skimming and scanning are of *low* importance (at this point); phoneme/grapheme: consonants may be of *some* concern; and sight vocabulary, phoneme/grapheme: vowels, vocabulary in context, and word part clues are of *high* concern. Performance on the reading comprehension test, upon which the instructional reading level is based, always is of instructional significance.

Two other tables aid the interpretation of the test scores in a level. One table suggests whether skills tested at a particular level should be retaught, practiced, or simply applied based upon raw scores. A second table, for the rate of comprehension test, uses raw score data to suggest that a student's rate of comprehension is: highly efficient; efficient—low rate; efficient—lower comprehension; inefficient—low rate; or inefficient—low comprehension.

The Norms Booklet and Manual for Interpreting test scores contain sufficient information for a user to score and interpret student performance in norm- and criterion-referenced terms. However, scoring and interpreting test data require a substantial amount of time and effort to accomplish, even when hand scoring keys are purchased. Consequently, machine scoring and interpretation services are available at an additional cost.

All RDT levels have booklets which can be hand and machine scored. There are consumable test booklets at every level and hand-scorable answer documents (sheets) at the Elementary, Intermediate, and Advanced 1 levels. Keys for scoring are an additional expense and require the purchase of the Norms Booklet as well. Though listed in the catalog, the Technical Manual is not presently available.

If the Psychological Corporation scores the tests, the subscriber receives two copies of the following reports: Pupil Objective Analysis for each student; Pupil Objective Analysis Summary for the class, the building, and the system level; and Class Instructional Report. These reports contain criterion-referenced information on subskill strengths and weaknesses, reading level, instructional importance (high, some, low) of subskills in light of reading level, and normative data relating individual students, classes, buildings and districts to local and national norms. The Class Instructional Report groups students by Instructional Reading Level. It also lists skill objectives tested, indicates how many students did not attain the criterion for each objective, and lists those students' names alphabetically. Additional scoring services, useful for administrators, offer summary and frequency data and local norms conversion tables.

Finally, the Manual for Interpreting contains tables pairing levels in seventeen basal series with estimates of instructional reading level. Separate resource guides for each basal series are also available that match the objectives of that series to the objectives on the MAT6 Achievement Tests. The information includes specific objectives listed as taught and practiced in the Teacher's Guide, workbook, and duplicating masters of the series.

Technical Aspects

The RDT Teacher's Manual for Interpreting has a section titled technical information. Here historical development of the MAT series is given, plus general information on how items were developed, selected, and refined. Information is also provided on norms, reliability, and validity of the RDT and the MAT6 Survey Battery.

The MAT6 is the sixth edition of the Metropolitan Achievement Tests, which first appeared in 1930 to 1932. The RDT was developed after "an exhaustive analysis of curriculum materials (nationwide) was performed" (p. 112). The most widely used basal readers were studied to determine objectives covered and the importance attributed to them. State curriculum guides, latest research, and publications of professional organizations in reading were reviewed. Approximately 40 experts in reading from around the country previewed the blueprints for the RDT. Items were developed, then subjected to a five stage review process by reading and measurement experts, a panel of minority educators, and 1,000 classroom teachers who helped field test the RDT. A Teacher Questionnaire was used to obtain information on the clarity of directions and items, artwork, format, and time to administer the tests. The RDT was standardized in the fall and spring of the 1984–85 school year. A total of 75,000 students in Grades K–9 participated; geographic region, school system size, socioeconomic index, and public and nonpublic schools were considered.

In order to have a continuous score scale across adjacent levels of the RDT, data obtained from the MAT6 Survey Battery were examined. The Reading Comprehension and Vocabulary tests of the Survey are identical to the Reading Comprehension and Vocabulary in Context Tests of the RDT. Based upon the performance of 6,000 students who took both the MAT6 Survey and RDT tests, with order of administration randomly assigned, estimates of difficulty were determined to be alike for adjacent levels of the RDT. Similar procedures were followed to make certain Forms L and M of the RDT for levels Primary 1 through Advanced 1 were equivalent. Alternate form reliability estimates for Rate of Comprehension, Skimming and Scanning, and Reading Comprehension range from .74 to .86 at the Intermediate Level (grades five and six), the level for which this reviewer had normative data. Internal consistency was assessed using the Kuder-Richardson Formula 20 (KR–20); at the Intermediate level, KR–20 estimates for the six tests in Forms L and M range from .79 to .98 (Total Reading score).

Validity was determined primarily in two ways. One, the opinions of reading experts and classroom teachers were used to check to content and the format of test items and test procedures against textbooks, other curricular materials, and current syllabuses and curriculum guides around the country. Two, 1,422 sixth grade students were administered both the MAT6 RDT and the *Otis-Lennon School Ability Test*, Form R. The OLSAT is designed specifically to assess school learning ability. Correlations between the RDT tests and the OLSAT range from a low of .33 (phoneme/grapheme: consonants) to .93 (reading comprehension). The correlation with the OLSAT and the Total RDT is .84.

Conclusions

The MAT6 Reading Diagnostic Tests are an impressive tool for diagnosing the reading strengths and weaknesses of elementary and junior high students. The test format and items have been carefully conceived and developed with the help of experts in reading, measurement specialists, educators sensitive to ethnic factors and handicapped persons in our society, editors, and many classroom teachers. An adequate sample of students, grades K–9, was taken to develop current normative data. Field testing also afforded ample teacher input on the test format, test clarity, and ease of use.

The reading skills and more global reading behaviors tested match the major strands found in most basal reading programs and district/state curricula. Some might find this unfortunate, since students' attitudes toward reading, interests in reading, and awareness of comprehension strategies are not a focus of assessment. However, reading diagnostic tests have traditionally been developed as group and individual measures of a more formalized character. Interview techniques, questionnaires, conferencing, and daily observations—procedures also of value for assessing reading—afford opportunities to gain information of a more subjective character than do paper and pencil tests like the RDT. One would expect that using the RDT in conjunction with these other, more informal measures, would provide a satisfactory profile of the reading progress of most students.

The diagnostic, criterion-referenced description of the RDT implies that skill clusters within tests include sufficient items to be reliable measures of the sub-skills listed. Many objectives, however, are tested with as few as three items, making conclusions about a student's performance reaching, or not reaching, criterion open to interpretation. On the Reading Comprehension Test the authors have appropriately stated that "separate objectives (listed) on the Reading Comprehension Test do not represent separate skills of reading" (p. 27). Test users who approach the teaching of reading comprehension through a skills orientation may find it helpful to analyze performance by objective, but they should not consider the information on performance to criterion, by objective, as the only or even best way to develop an instructional program for reading comprehension. It was refreshing to discover that the RDT contains numerous teaching tips and tables for interpreting the significance of test scores. Great care is taken to explain the uses and restrictions of each type of score.

Test users are encouraged to weigh the significance of lower test performance in light of overall instructional reading level (IRL). Students who are reading well may not require remedial instruction in some of the decoding areas tested as low; conversely, students not yet decoding reasonably fluently may forego instruction on reading rate until their reading fluency improves. Unfortunately, cautionary statements about the use of scores is not extended to estimates of instructional reading level, in which the authors seem to place great significance. While this is not unique to the RDT, but is a factor whenever graded passages are used, the issue does warrant some attention in the Manual for Interpreting. Passage difficulty on the Reading Comprehension Test was determined by using only one of two popular readability formulas. In a further attempt to level text passages length, difficulty of concepts and interest level of passage topics were equated to texts found in basal readers. Instructional reading level is defined as that grade level at which 70 percent of the passage questions are answered correctly; independent reading level is 90 percent comprehension; and frustration level is that grade level at which 50 percent or less of the passage questions are answered correctly.

Though the authors mention the importance of a reader's background knowledge, kinds of thinking a reader does while reading, and the importance of reading for specific purposes, test users are not told to consider seriously these factors when interpreting a student's overall reading level. Based on instructional reading level, low scores on the remaining tests in a level are judged to be of high, some, or low instructional importance. What if the IRL is invalid for a student because of his or her background, test-taking ability, or focus (thinking) while reading a particular passage? Won't conclusions about skill strengths and weaknesses be invalid because the basis for judgment, namely estimates of passage difficulty, are equally invalid for this student? The authors have made an attempt to influence purpose for reading by including a prereading question with each passage—a heavily touted feature new to the MAT6 RDT. But, who is to say that a student will even read these questions during testing when they realize that the tests are timed? A more strenuous effort is needed, as has been done with stating limitations for types of norm-referenced scores, to warn test users against accepting estimates of students' reading levels, especially to form three or four reading groups in a classroom, without observing daily how students read in their regular textbooks. More, too, should be mentioned about students of the same IRL who have different skill strengths and weaknesses. It appears that test users might interpret IRL as *the* criterion for grouping students for reading, a common practice that the Manual for Interpreting seems to validate (p. 24) despite research evidence to the contrary.

Cost factors may be an issue for many users of the RDT. Several sittings are needed to administer the entire battery, yet the data refer to reading only and not the range of subjects tested on an achievement test. The average teacher might well balk at the time and effort needed to hand score the battery for an entire class of students, yet find the time delay created by sending the tests off to be machine scored unacceptable because the results cannot be used to plan instruction right away. While this delay would not impact as much on building, district, and state use of the test results, teachers might resent the instructional time devoted to testing if the results cannot be used to teach while students still need help in the areas identified.

Besides time needed to score the RDT, there is a substantial financial investment as well. It would cost between $95 and $120 to purchase materials for a class in which the tests are hand scored, and $175 or more to have the same materials machine scored. For the data received, the costs seem reasonable, but a regular classroom teacher might not utilize the wealth of diagnostic information if she or he perceives that most students are meeting or exceeding grade level norms. It is more likely that reading specialists and resource teachers would act on much of the information provided in the RDT and even be willing to hand score the tests in order to have that information right away.

In summary, the RDT is an excellent diagnostic tool. Carefully conceived, thoroughly tested, and broad in scope, it is a test worth considering for classroom and clinic when a paper and pencil measure of reading is acceptable. Not all the important objectives of reading are examined, but in conjunction with more informal, on-going measures of reading processes, skills, attitudes, and interests, it should help the informed teacher develop an accurate profile of reading strengths and weaknesses for most students.

Stanford Diagnostic Reading Test

Authors: Bjorn Karlsen and Eric F. Gardner

Publisher: Harcourt Brace Jovanovich

Edition: Third

Copyright: 1984

Reviewer: Gary W. Bates, Ohio University

General Description

There are four levels of the *Stanford Diagnostic Reading Test* (SDRT) with two forms at each level, allowing for pre- and posttesting. The following are available for each level: Directions for Administering, Manual for Interpreting, Norms Booklet, Instructional Placement Report, Hand Scorable Booklet Keys, and Handbook of Instructional Techniques and Materials.

The *Stanford Diagnostic Reading Test* is intended as a diagnostic instrument to identify the pupil's strengths and weaknesses and therefore places emphasis on the low achiever. It is not recommended for gifted pupils or superior readers.

☐ Description of Subtests and What They Measure

Auditory Vocabulary (Red, Green, Brown). The words in this subtest include the various parts of speech and represent three general content areas: reading and literature, mathematics and science, and social studies and the arts. All items are dictated to pupils, so the subtest provides information about the pupil's language competence without requiring them to read.

Auditory Discrimination (Red, Green). Auditory discrimination has to do with the ability to hear similarities and differences among sounds in words and is considered by some to be a prerequisite to the acquisition of the visual decoding skills.

Phonetic Analysis (Red, Green, Brown, Blue). Phonetic analysis has to do with relationships between sounds and letters (phoneme-grapheme relationships). For each item in this subtest, pupils were asked to determine particular sounds in letters or words and match each sound to the letter or letters, or to a common or variant spelling of that sound.

Word Reading (Red). This subtest assesses the pupil's ability to recognize words and their meaning. The authors feel this is an assessment of "applied" reading for pupils who cannot read sentences or paragraphs. Students are asked to identify words that describe a particular illustration.

Reading Comprehension (Red). Reading comprehension is assessed at the Red Level by means of sentences and short reading passages. In Part A, students are asked to identify a picture that best illustrates the meaning of printed sentences or riddles. Part B measures the student's ability to read and comprehend short passages presented in a multiple-choice cloze format.

Reading Comprehension (Green, Brown, Blue). For the green level, literal and inferential comprehension are assessed by both "short reading passages presented in a multiple-choice cloze format and by short passages followed by questions." For the brown and blue levels short reading passages followed by questions are used.

Structural Analysis (Green, Brown, Blue). This subtest measures the student's facility with structural analysis or the ability to decode words through the analysis of word parts, such as syllables, affixes, and root words.

Reading Rate/Fast Reading (Brown, Blue). Reading Rate measures the pupil's ability to read easy materials quickly and with comprehension.

Vocabulary (Blue). Words included in this subtest were selected from lists of words most commonly encountered in the high school curriculum. Approximately equal numbers of words from the areas of reading and literature, mathematics and science, and social studies were selected. Sentences containing each word were written to reflect the particular subject area from which the word was chosen.

Word Parts (Blue). This subtest assesses the pupil's knowledge of such word parts as prefixes, suffixes, root words, and word roots.

Scanning and Skimming (Blue). In Part A "students are presented with a set of questions and are asked to find the answers in the accompanying article, without reading the article through completely....In Part B, students are asked to extract both general and specific information about an article in a short period of time."

The following table (Table 4) contains administration time and internal consistency reliability estimates for each subtest at each level.

		Administration Time in Minutes	KR-20
Table 4			
Administration Time and Internal Consistency			
Reliabilty of Subtests			
Red Level[a]:	Auditory Vocabulary	20	.79
	Auditory Discrimination	15	.91
	Phonetic Analysis	20	.88
	Word Reading	15	.91
	Reading Comprehension	20	.93
		15	
	[a]KR for Grade 2 only		
Green Level[b]:	Auditory Vocabulary	20	.84
	Auditory Discrimination	20	.91
	Phonetic Analysis	20	.87
	Structural Analysis	12	.92
		12	
	Reading Comprehension	30	.94 T
			.88 L
			.89 I
	[b]KR for Grade 3 only		
Brown Level[c]:	Auditory Vocabulary	20	.87
	Reading Comprehension	40	.94 T
			.88 L
			.89 I
	Phonetic Analysis	15	.90
	Structural Analysis	15	.94
		15	
	Reading Rate	3	—
	[c]KR for Grade 5 only		

T = Total;   L = Literal;   I = Inferential

		Administration Time in Minutes	KR-20
Table 4 (con't) Administration Time and Internal Consistency Reliabilty of Subtests			
Blue Level[d]:	Reading Comprehension	40	.92 T .88 L .84 I
	Vocabulary	15	.86
	Word Parts	15	.78
	Phonetic Analysis	12	.92
	Structural Analysis	12	.72
	Scanning and Skimming	8 11	—
	Fast Reading	3	—
	[d]KR for Grade 9 only		

T = Total;   L = Literal;   I = Inferential

Technical Aspects

☐ Reliability

The reliability of a test is the extent to which a test yields consistent results. Two types of reliability are normally considered, internal consistency—are the items in a subtest consistent in what they measure? And test-retest reliability—do the subtests measure consistently over time? Test-retest reliability is the most important in terms of making instructional decisions based upon test results.

Kuder-Richardson Formula 20 (KR–20) was used to determine the internal consistency reliability of SDRT scores. KR–20 scores for fall testing are summarized in Table 4. Scores for only one grade level are reported here, although the Norms Booklet for each level contains KR–20 reliability scores for each intended grade level. The internal consistency reliability correlations reported for each grade level for each form of the SDRT are very good, showing that the items in any given subtest tend to be consistent in what they measure. The booklets for each level states that KR–20 scores for spring testing are available upon request. There are no test-retest reliability scores reported and this is a serious omission.

☐ Validity

The validity of a test is the degree to which the test measures what it is intended to measure. A common way to determine validity is to compute correlations between the test under consideration and a well-known or generally accepted test of a particular skill. The raw subtest scores on the various forms of the SDRT have been compared to the raw subtest scores of the *Otis-Lennon School Ability Test*. The reported intercorrelations vary from a low of .24 to a high of .97 for different raw scores of different subtests at different levels. In other words, sometimes the SDRT subtests measure a similar skill to subtests of the *Otis-Lennon*, but it depends upon the raw score and the level of the SDRT being compared. The norms booklets recommend that school districts examine the test's content and compare it to their local reading objectives to determine if the SDRT measures what the local reading curriculum emphasizes. This is good advice and the only way to determine local validity of any test.

☐ Test Development

Based upon the information provided in the norms booklets, the revision of the SDRT seems to have followed ideal test development procedures. Test specifications and objectives were developed for each level, new items were pilot-tested with approximately 100,000 students from 50 school systems balanced for socioeconomic status, geographic region, and school-system enrollment. Based upon the pilot-test data, items were selected for the final forms of the tests which were then standardized on another national stratified random sample consisting of approximately 30,000 students in grades two through twelve from 33 school systems. Demographic characteristics of students in the national standardization sample are provided in the norms booklet for each level.

Conclusions

The *Stanford Diagnostic Reading Test* appears to be a useful test for its intended audience—low achieving readers. The directions for administering the tests are clear and easy to follow. The availability of hand scorable answer sheets allows schools or school districts to reduce their assessment budgets. The handbooks of instructional techniques and materials provide suggestions for grouping students in up to eight groups based upon the diagnostic findings.

The philosophy underlying the *Stanford Diagnostic Reading Test* "assumes that the reading characteristics of students can be diagnosed and that prescriptive instruction should be carried out in the specific areas in which students are having difficulty." The approach to skills instruction is closer to skills-in-isolation than to whole language instruction. However, specific instructional techniques and materials are suggested for each of the subtests and for each of the diagnostic groups for each level of the test. A good creative teacher could incorporate the suggestions into any type of reading program.

Although the handbooks do warn that test reliability is subject to considerable error when referring to individual diagnosis, it bears repeating: diagnostic inferences based upon findings from the SDRT are more reliable for *groups* than for *individuals*. With that in mind, it is clear that the issue of reliability remains the most crucial for the SDRT—reliability of individual scores and test-retest reliability. The publisher would be wise to make the group test-retest reliability coefficients available to anyone who has purchased the test.

ADULT READING TESTS

Introduction

Since the advent of the industrial age, business leaders, politicians, citizen action groups, and educators have been interested in helping adult learners to acquire basic literacy skills. A number of reading tests have gained in popularity over the past decade which focus on adult reading ability. Three tests have been included in this section which have captured much of the present adult reading assessment market. Several questions regarding the efficacy and validity of these and other adult reading measures are offered for the reader's consideration.

1. What philosophy of reading has been applied to the adult reader by the test authors?
2. What is the nature of reading passages and exercises used in the instrument? Are they appropriate in terms of interest level and content?
3. Who is intended audience (e.g., college freshmen, illiterate adults, etc.)?
4. Is this a norm-referenced test? If so, does the norm group match the intended student(s) in terms of socio-economic considerations?
5. Is the test intended for diagnostic assessment? If so, to what extent can the examiner gain useful information for classroom decision-making?

Degrees of Reading Power (DRP)*

Developer: The College Board, New York State Education Department and
Touchstone Applied Science Associates (TASA)

Publisher: The College Board

Edition: First

Copyright: 1980

Reviewer: Marino C. Alvarez, Tennessee State University

The *Degrees of Reading Power* (DRP) was developed by the College Board,
in conjunction with the New York State Education Department, the Carnegie
Corporation, and Touchstone Applied Science Associates, Inc. (TASA). The DRP
is designed to measure student reading comprehension. It is a program that aims
to integrate assessment and instruction in reading, to monitor student progress,
and to provide an outcome measure for school accountability. There are three
components to this program: (1) tests to measure the student's ability to comprehend
nonfiction English prose; (2) readability analyses of instructional materials; and (3)
instructional support materials and services (*DRP Handbook*, 1986, p. 1). The DRP
was developed to place nonfictional materials of varying difficulty levels and student
reading comprehension test scores on the same scale.

General Description

Each DRP test consists of prose passages based on nonfictional subject matter.
DRP tests are untimed. The passages are untitled and each contain approximately
325 words. They are arranged in test booklets starting with less difficult selections and progressing to more difficult levels. The passages are modified versions of a cloze test in that there are seven sentences within each selection that
contain one deletion designated by a blank space. Each deletion has five word
choices from which the examinee is to select the most appropriate word that
relates to the information in the sentence.

The DRP tests are criterion-referenced measures. They can be administered
as either a group or individual instrument, and are described as appropriate for
students: in heterogeneous classes; Chapter I; special education; gifted and tal-
ented; those for whom English is a second language; and those in adult education
programs. The DRP consists of reusable test booklets for grades three through
twelve and are available in two alternate series, PA and PB. There is a third
series, CP, available for college placement testing.

---

* The editor acknowledges that the DRP is a widely used instrument in public and private
schools, as well as with adults.

The DRP test has practice materials that are to be used to acquaint the examinee with the test format. The practice test, form PX–1, is a consumable test, consisting of three passages with 21 test items. The practice test, form PX–1, can be used to estimate which DRP test form is best suited for either an entire class or an individual student. The *DRP Handbook* (1986) recommends averaging the number of correct items that a group (class) of students obtained on form PX–1 to select the appropriate test for students. To test students individually, it is suggested that student placement with a test be made according to items scored correctly on the PX–1 test using these criteria: 6–8 correct items, use PA–8 or PB–8; 9–10 correct items, use PA–6 or PB–6; 11–14 correct items, use PA–4 or PB–4; 15–21 items correct, use PA–2 or PB–2. The recommended guidelines for the selection of the test for groups that are heterogeneous in reading ability are PA–8 and PB–8, grades 3–5, contains 8 passages with 56 test items; PA–6 and PB–6, grades 5–7, contains 11 passages with 77 test items; PA–4 and PB–4, grades 7–9, contains 11 passages with 77 test items, PA–2 and PB–2, grades 9–12, contains 11 passages with 77 test items, and CP–1A and CP–1B, grades 12–14, contains 9 passages with 63 test items. The *DRP Handbook* (1986) advises that "local judgment" should be used when selecting the test form for grades that overlap such as five, seven, and nine.

The DRP program is based on a readability formula developed by Bormuth (1969) to measure reading ease or difficulty of both test and instructional materials. This readability scale of measurement is referred to as DRP units. The scale ranges in reading ease from approximately 30 DRP units (easy) to approximately 85 DRP units (difficult). These DRP units are used to determine student placement in materials with similar DRP unit ratings. Like the traditional cloze test, three reading levels are obtained from this test. First, the independent level is the level at which the student is able to answer at least 90 percent of the questions correctly. Next, there is the instructional level, at which the student answers 75 percent of the questions correctly. Finally, the frustration level is the one at which the student can answer only 50 percent of the questions correctly. These three reading levels are used as an index for assigning reading materials according to student reading ability. Using the raw-score results of the DRP test, a student's range of probability (P) for these three levels are: Independent (P = .90), Instructional (P = .80, P = .75, P = .70 with .75 being the midpoint), and Frustration (P = .50).

☐ Testing Materials

The *DRP Handbook* (1986) gives clear directions for a separate preparation and administration of the test. This is to provide ample time for students to complete the untimed test within 50 minutes or, if needed, to extend this time so that all students can be given an opportunity to complete the test without time constraints. It is during the preparation session that students are given the practice test, form PX–1. The DRP Test Answer Sheets are also to be completed during this stage. It is during the actual test administration that the completed preliminary items appearing on the DRP Test Answer Sheets are then distributed to the students followed by the DRP test booklets.

Each step of the preparation and administration stages are clearly written for the examiner to follow. The conversion tables show how raw scores are transformed to DRP scores at five different levels of comprehension. These five levels correspond with those mentioned above. These tables are not difficult to use.

DRP tests can either be hand scored using scoring stencils, or machine scored using the services provided by the College Board. These services include an Alphabetical Class Roster that provides each student's raw score; independent, instructional, and frustration levels in DRP units; and a rank order grade roster. There is also a Summary Statistics Report for class, school, and district, a National Percentile Rank, and other optional services such as student labels, raw score summary, item response summary, and research tapes.

The College Board has available a Readability Analysis Service to analyze the readability of instructional materials. Readability Report, or its Supplement, can be obtained through using the Readability Analysis Service which lists the difficulty level of published textbooks. Readability of these textbooks are given in DRP units. Also available is *Micra DRP*, a software program for microcomputers, that gives an approximation of DRP readability levels for locally developed materials, library resources, and other materials that are not mentioned in the *Readability Report*. This software is currently available for the Apple II+, IIe, and IIc, and for the IBM-PC. In addition, there are consultant services that are available to help integrate a reading in the content areas program. In essence, the DRP program can be used as a strand in a reading in the content area school program.

Technical Aspects

Technical information concerning the DRP tests is contained in the *DRP Handbook* (1986) and in the technical manual for the DRP entitled *The DRP: An Effectiveness Measure in Reading* (1987). The reliability and validity of the DRP have been determined from a sample of 32,242 students in grades three through nine in an urban school system. The technical manual presents data from studies that show (1) DRP tests homogeneous with low standard of error measurements, (2) alternate form reliability, (3) a comparison of DRP test data to the Rasch model, (4) reliability of replicate DRP measurements over time, and (5) gain score reliability.

To test for homogeneity and standard error of measurement, DRP tests PA–2, PA–4, PA–6, and PA–8 were given to a sample of 32,242 students in grades three through twelve in an urban school system. The KR–20 coefficients are high ranging from $r = .93$ to $r = .97$, indicating that DRP tests are homogeneous. The standard errors of measurement are low ranging from 3.0 to 3.6. Students in grade (N = 353) four and grade six (N = 250) were used to test alternate forms reliability. Estimates ranged from .86 to .91. The sample selection for this study was from schools with enrollments of minority students varying between 20 and 80 percent. DRP test data compare to the Rasch model when students are in the effective range of the test (students scoring between 25 percent and 75 percent of the items correctly). Standard errors of Rasch ability are approximately 2.5 DRP units. A study to determine the reliability of DRP tests over time and gain score reliability was conducted with a statewide sample of 1,969 students in grade four and 2,231 students in grade six indicated that the DRP tests are reliable. Pretest/posttest correlations were: grade four, r = .83 and grade six, r = .88 when equal test forms were given five months apart.

The reliability of the DRP seems to be in order for the target sample and the test forms used. A systematic approach to validation has been followed (Carver, 1985a, 1985b; Linn, 1981; Kibby, 1981). The elimination of grade equivalents are in line with IRA 1981 delegate recommendations and its control of item difficulty indicates progress in attempting to link student reading ability with instructional reading materials. There are, however, several factors that need to be considered. Schools with less than 20 percent of minority students were not used in the study. As Kibby (1981) notes, minority populations with less than 20 percent living in suburban and rural communities were excluded from the statewide sample which may have had an effect on the results. A related issue is that there is insufficient socioeconomic data for participating students. Also DRP tests are limited to nonfiction English prose; therefore, no judgments can be made as to student reading effectiveness in fiction and poetry.

An area of contention seems to be in the claim that DRP tests can be used to match materials to students with varying reading abilities. The DRP degree difficulty of a passage is determined from using the surface features of a passage (word familiarity, average word length, and average sentence length). From an empirical view, Carver (1985a) found DRP units to be reasonably reliable and valid. However, in a separate study Carver (1985b) reported that the DRP test is inconsistent across ability levels when forecasting textbooks that can be matched to students. He stated that the DRP underestimates the difficulty of materials for the typical or average student in the elementary grades (3–5), accurately estimates the reading ability of the typical student in middle grades (6–9), and overestimates the difficulty of materials for the typical student in the upper grades (10–12). In a study with third- and fifth-grade students that involved the use of the DRP test, Duffelmeyer and Adamson (1986) reported that the DRP underestimates the reading ability of students reading at the fifth-grade level and below. Their findings concurred with Carver's (1985a). Rankin (1986) refuted Carver's (1985a, 1985b) findings and reported that several factors of the DRP program were not considered (e.g., nature of the reading construct being measured; operational definitions of independent, instructional, and frustration reading levels; the use of other reading levels in addition to instructional for book selection). Instead, Rankin suggested that the DRP program be evaluated as a total entity that includes student test scores, readability values, and professional judgments.

Conclusions

The DRP test seems to be a valid instrument when used to: (1) compare students with each other in reading achievement; (2) measure gain in reading ability; and (3) indicate remedial assistance. However, further study needs to be conducted to show that forecasting in DRP units can be matched effectively with students across varying reading abilities. There is some evidence that the DRP test is less reliable at forecasting materials for the student who scores below grade nine and above grade nine (Bormuth, 1985; Carver, 1985a, 1985b; Duffelmeyer & Adamson, 1986; Rankin, 1986).

The DRP program seems to be a significant step forward in matching reading material to readers, but DRP scores should not be the sole indicator used in selecting books (Rankin, 1986). Klare (1984) suggests several warnings when dealing with readability formulas, one of which is not to rely on formulas alone when selecting reading materials, but, instead, to take into consideration factors that these readability formulas cannot predict. This particular warning seems highly relevant to the DRP test and its ability to forecast.

Readability formulas are *estimates* of passage difficulty. While the *DRP Handbook* (1986) and *The DRP: An Effectiveness Measure in Reading* (1987) acknowledge the uses and abuses of readability formulas, there are serious conditions associated with factors not measured by readability formulas that are not easily addressed by any test based on a readability index. For example, while surface features of a text can be measured, other text characteristics such as concept load, meaningful headings and subheadings, definition of key vocabulary, and sequencing of materials are some important factors not measured by readability formulas in the selection of materials. Reader background, experience, interest, and motivation are other key factors not accounted for in the DRP readability index. A test of this nature that relies on a readability assessment is subject to the factors not measured by readability formulas.

The DRP test can be used as a screening instrument and to estimate reading materials (within limits). It is important to bear in mind that teacher judgment is a vital ingredient of the DRP program to maximize its effectiveness. The need for teachers to be informed about the issues of readability are vital when selecting materials for students of varying reading ability. Several sources are listed in the references for interested readers (e.g., Davison, 1988; Farr & Carey, 1986; Fry, 1988; Klare, 1984, 1988; Johnston, 1983, 1984).

References

Bormuth, J. R. (1985). A response to "Is the Degrees of Reading Power test valid or invalid?" *Journal of Reading* 29, 42–47.

Bormuth, J. R. (1969, March). *Development of readability analyses.* Final Report, Project No. 7-0052, Contract No. OEG-3-7-070052-0326, Office of Education, Bureau of Research, U.S. Department of Health, Education and Welfare.

Carver, R. P. (1985a). Measuring readability using DRP units. *Journal of Reading Behavior* 17, 303–16.

Carver, R. P. (1985b). Is the Degrees of Reading Power test valid or invalid? *Journal of Reading* 29, 34–41.

Davison, A. (1988). Assigning grade levels without formulas: Some case studies. In B. L. Zakaluk and S. J. Samuels (Eds.), *Readability: Its past, present, and future* (pp. 36–45). Newark, DE: International Reading Association.

DRP handbook. (1986). New York: College Entrance Examination Board.

Duffelmeyer, F. A., and Adamson, S. (1986). Matching students with instructional level materials using the *Degrees of Reading Power System, Reading Research and Instruction* 25, 192–200.

Farr, R., and Carey, R. F. (1986). *Reading: What can be measured?* (2nd ed.). Newark, DE: International Reading Association.

Fry, E. B. (1988). Writeability: The principles of writing for increased comprehension. In B. L. Zakaluk and S. J. Samuels (Eds.), *Readability: Its past, present, and future* (pp. 77–95). Newark, DE: International Reading Association.

Johnston, P. H. (1984). Assessment in reading. In P. D. Pearson (Ed.), *Handbook of reading research,* (pp. 147–82) Chapter 6. New York: Longman.

Johnston, P. H. (1983). *Reading comprehension assessment: A cognitive basis.* Newark, DE: International Reading Association.

Kibby, M. W. (1981). The degrees of reading power. *Journal of Reading* 24, 416–27.

Klare, G. R. (1984). Readability. In P. D. Pearson (Ed). *Handbook of reading research,* Chapter 22 (pp. 681–744). New York: Longman.

Klare, G. R. (1988). The formative years. In B. L. Zakaluk and S. J. Samuels (Eds.). *Readability: Its past, present, and future* (pp. 14–34). Newark, DE: International Reading Association.

Koslin, B. L.; Zeno, S.; and Koslin, S. (1987). *The DRP: An effectiveness measure in reading.* New York: College Entrance Examination Board.

Linn, R. L. (1981). Issues of validity for criterion-referenced measures. *Applied Psychological Measurement* 4, 547–61.

Rankin, E. F. (1986). The validity of the Degrees of Reading Power Test: A response to Carver's critique. *North Central Reading Association Yearbook* 13, 165–88.

Readability report in DRP units (7th ed.). (1985). New York: College Entrance Examination Board.

Reading Research Quarterly. (1981). Resolutions passed by Delegates Assembly—April 1981, 16.

Tests of Adult Basic Education, Forms 5 and 6

Author: CTB/McGraw-Hill

Publisher: CTB/McGraw-Hill

Edition: Third

Copyright: 1987

Reviewer: E. Sutton Flynt, Pittsburg State University

General Description

The *Tests of Adult Basic Education, Forms 5 and 6* (TABE), touted as "the most widely used tests for adult basic skills in the world," are standardized, norm-referenced tests that assess achievement in reading, mathematics, language, and spelling. The complete battery is composed of seven subtests and is provided at four overlapping levels. The levels and estimated grade level ranges are: level E (easy) 2.6-4.9, level M (medium) 4.6-6.9, level D (difficult) 6.6-8.9, and level A (advanced) 8.6-12.9. In addition to the complete battery the publisher provides a Practice Exercise for examinees who might have difficulty with the mechanics of taking a standardized test. A Locator Test, composed of 25 vocabulary and 25 math items, is provided to determine which of the four levels of the TABE to administer to a particular examinee. For instance, where no prior information is known about an individual the Survey Form of the TABE, an abbreviated version of Form 5, is available for use as an initial screening and general placement instrument.

The TABE, according to its publisher, can be utilized to gather preinstructional information about an individual's ability in the four basic skill areas tested, to assess growth in discrete skills via a pretest and posttest scenario, to develop individualized instructional programs, and to provide the learner with evidence of his or her ability. Although designed to assist in diagnosing and placing examinees in adult education programs, an additional use with this most recent edition of the TABE is its use to predict the performance of examinees on the test of *General Educational Development* (GED).

Reading achievement is measured by a Vocabulary subtest that consists of 30 items and a Comprehension subtest of 40 items based on passages read by the examinee. The Vocabulary subtest requires the examinee to identify appropriate synonyms and antonyms for targeted words, select the appropriate meaning of suffixes and prefixes, choose the appropriate word that has the same meaning suggested by two phrases, select the word that correctly completes a sentence with a blank, and, in levels D and A, select the appropriate word for blanks in a modified cloze passage. The Comprehension subtest assesses comprehension of reading passages centered around the subskills of reading for details, characterization, main ideas, and inferring events described in passages. Except for no poetry at level E, the passages at each level of the TABE include at least one example of a letter, an advertisement, a poem, and an information article. The Test Coordinators Handbook provided by the publisher states that the comprehension subtest also assesses the ability to differentiate various forms of writing and various writing techniques.

Mathematics ability is measured by two subtests. The Mathematics Computation subtest contains 48 items related to the four basic mathematical operations. The content of this subtest varies according to the level of the TABE administered but includes whole numbers, fractions, decimals, algebraic expressions, percents, and exponents. The Mathematics Concepts and Applications subtest has 40 items related to numeration, number sentences, number theory, problem solving, measurement, and geometry.

Language achievement is measured by a 30-item Language Mechanics subtest and a 45-item Language Expression subtest. The former focuses primarily on capitalization and punctuation in both sentences and passages. The short passages attempt to measure the examinee's editing skills. The latter requires the examinee to select the appropriate part of speech to complete a sentence, to identify complete sentences, to choose the sentence that best combines two underlined sentences, to select the best topic sentence that fits a given paragraph, and to identify the correct sequence of a series of sentences.

Spelling ability is measured by a 30-item Spelling subtest. Each item consists of a sentence with a blank and four different spellings to choose from to correctly fill the blank.

Technical Aspects

The TABE was tried out and normed during the first five months of 1986. Over 7000 individuals from four different reference groups, namely, adult basic education programs, adult offender programs, juvenile offender programs, and vocational/technical training programs, were used to establish norms and select items. From this effort, as well as an equating study between Forms 5 and 6 and Forms 3 and 4 of a previous TABE edition, data were obtained to establish correlations between TABE performance and performance on the GED. This latter point, using the TABE to predict the probability of GED performance, is of significance to individuals who administer or teach in many adult education programs because often the bottom line goal for many enrollees is to successfully pass the GED. The correlations between the GED and the TABE are provided in Table 5.

Table 5 CORRELATIONS ESTABLISHED BETWEEN GED AND TABE		
GED TEST	**TABE TEST**	**CORRELATION**
Writing	Total Language	.55
Social Studies	Total Language	.63
Science	Total Language	.60
Reading	Total Language	.64
Math	Total Language	.64
Average	Total Language	.70

Reliability for the TABE was established using the Kuder-Richardson formula 20 (KR–20). Reliability coefficients for each of the four reference groups are provided in the technical report manual by level. In general the reported reliability coefficients were in the high 80s or low 90s for all subtests except for the Language Mechanics subtest which consistently had coefficients in the 70s or low 80s.

Validity information provided by the publisher centered around content validity and efforts to reduce bias. The content validity of the TABE results from efforts to examine current curricular guides from various adult education programs throughout the country, along with recently published textbooks and instructional programs. Basic skills common to the aforementioned sources were compared to the objectives of published achievement tests. Coupling this tactic with experienced teachers as item and passage writers, readability formulas, and vocabulary controls, the TABE's content was developed. The procedures for reducing bias included having professionals in the education community consider and comment on passages and items related to language and subject matter and developing a bias index for each item.

The performance of individuals on the TABE is reported by stanine, percentile rank, and grade equivalents. With respect to grade equivalent information, grade equivalents are based on the *California Achievement Tests E and F* standardization administrations. That is, a grade equivalent reported for the TABE represents the grade and month in school of students in the *California Achievement Tests* norm group whose performance is equivalent to the test performance of the TABE examinee.

Besides providing norm-referenced scores, the publisher also provides something called "objective mastery scores." The TABE purports to measure 48 major category objectives, thereby enabling the reporting of whether or not a specific objective or skill has been mastered.

Conclusions

The 1987 version of the TABE is a marked improvement over earlier versions because of the attention given by the publisher to aspects of the test such as the norming group, content validity, the objectives/skill performance report, and the possibility of estimating an individual's probability of successfully passing the GED. However, these improvements are also, in part, liabilities if not fully understood by the test coordinator, examiners, and instructors that work with and for adult-education students. The publisher has provided detailed information and warnings about misuses regarding this instrument in the Test Coordinators Manual and the Technical Report, both of which should be read and carefully studied before wholesale use of the TABE.

Detailed norming information is provided in the technical report by the publisher. Subsequently, if a test coordinator examines the norm group, it becomes apparent that the percent of representation by the four reference groups is not equally distributed. The approximate representation by each of the reference groups is: adult basic education students (33 percent), adult offenders (52 percent), juvenile offenders (7 percent), and vocational/technical students (8 percent). Additionally, ethnic representation in the combined norming sample was 44 percent black, 13 percent hispanic, 6 percent asian, and 36 percent other. Only 29 percent of the norming sample were female. The conclusion from this data suggests that individuals in certain educational settings should study the norming sample carefully and decide if their enrollees can legitimately be compared with norming groups of the TABE.

The content of the reading passages of the TABE, developed by teachers and other professionals associated with adult learning centers, was based on identified common basic skills of instructional programs, curriculum guides, and current textbooks related to adult education. However, the resulting subtests related to reading include such objectives as character analysis, inferencing the tone or mood of a passage, and differentiating between forms of writing. Very little attention is given to the idea of "reading to do" or "reading to learn," even at higher levels.

The content of the passages is questionable as well. The idea of having adults—whose primary concern often is to improve their employment situation—read poetry and passages about Greek gods and animals is not readily justifiable. More of the passages should be related to adult topics, needs, and interests, and they should address the idea of functioning in the real world more directly.

The implication by the publisher that the TABE has criterion reference potential via the objectives performance report is also an area that warrants scrutiny. If an adult education center's objectives match those of the TABE, then this aspect may prove valuable; however, if what the center's curriculum teaches does not relate specifically to these reading and language objectives, then the value of the objectives performance report is of little value.

The final comment related to the TABE's liabilities has to do with predicting GED performance. The publisher makes an effort to warn test coordinators about the type of student that might benefit from this type of information but, regardless, the correlations are low and additional testing of an individual might be unnecessary if the adult program in question has much of the material available for GED preparation.

In summary, the TABE will continue to have a prominent place in adult education programs in this country. It is one of few instruments of its type, and as the adult population in need of training continues to grow for a variety of reasons, the TABE's use will grow. Many of the individuals currently working in adult educational settings like the TABE and feel comfortable with what it provides them regarding individual ability and need. Consequently, individuals who consult with adult education centers, individuals who train the professionals that staff such centers, and the administrators of such centers need to educate users of tests such as the TABE so that both the benefits and limitations of this type of test are known and understood.

The Nelson-Denny Reading Test

Authors: James I. Brown, J. Michael Bennett, and Gerald Hanna

Publisher: The Riverside Publishing Company

Edition: Forms E and F

Copyright: 1981

Reviewers: Rosemarie J. Park and Rebecca Olson Storlie, University of Minnesota

General Description

The *Nelson-Denny* is a reading test designed for high school and college level students. The test contains three major elements: reading vocabulary, reading comprehension, and reading rate.

The test can be administered either individually or in groups. The format is standard multiple-choice with a separate answer sheet provided. The vocabulary subtest allows 15 minutes for completion and the comprehension and rate subtests each allow 20 minutes. There are two equivalent forms, E and F, of this test.

The vocabulary test is extensive with 100 items asking the student to select the correct response among five alternatives describing or defining the word given. The first part of the comprehension test is a brief test of reading rate that asks the student to mark the line in a preliminary paragraph completed at the end of 60 seconds. Some provision is made for those whose reading rate is much faster than this.

The remainder of the test consists of eight fairly lengthy selections from the humanities, social sciences, and sciences, followed by multiple-choice questions requiring students to select one of five completions to the sentence stem. Questions generally ask for recall of facts, inferential comprehension, and recognition of the main idea of each passage.

The self-scoring answer sheets give stanine scores for grades nine, ten, eleven, and twelve, and for two-year and four-year colleges. A separate table gives grade equivalent scores.

The test has three main uses according to the authors. First, the Nelson-Denny may be used as a screening instrument to determine whether a student could qualify for advance placement in courses or should be placed in a remedial reading class. Second, the test may be used to predict academic performance in college. Finally, the test may be used diagnostically by comparing variation in vocabulary, comprehension, and rate scores. Some suggested breakdown within each subtest is given to aid diagnosis. For example, vocabulary is broken down into words with prefixes and those without.

Technical Aspects

☐ Test Development

This test was standardized on public and parochial high school students and on two- and four-year college students. Vocabulary items were selected based primarily on their power to discriminate. Words were chosen from high school and college texts and popular periodicals.

Comprehension items, as with vocabulary, were selected primarily on their ability to discriminate. In addition, content validity was looked at both in relation to breadth of subject matter and comparability between the alternative forms of the test. Range in student ability was also considered when assigning difficulty level.

□ Reliability

Reliability reflects the degree to which a test is consistent. The overall reliability for this test using an alternative form method was .91. Most reliable, and in concordance with most such tests, was vocabulary at .92; least reliable was the reading rate at .69. The authors suggest that the reading rate scores be used for groups only and not to compute individual gain scores.

The Standard Error of Measurement is reported for grades 9–14 and, as reported, is greatest for the reading rate subtest.

□ Context Dependence

One additional and interesting item of data is given by the authors. A limited sample of 167 and 225 college students were given the comprehension test with and without the paragraphs on which the questions were based. This was designed to measure the extent to which the questions depended on the context information in the paragraphs. The study showed that students depended heavily on the context from the paragraphs to answer the questions, thus indicating the desired outcome for any test.

A summary of the descriptive and reliability data is given in Table 6.

Table 6
Forms E and F
Descriptive and Reliability Data for Equating Sample

			Grades					
			9	10	11	12	13	14
Vocabulary		n	409	438	387	343	165	74
		r	.89	.89	.91	.93	.95	.93
	Form E	M	27.6	32.3	34.4	38.9	55.8	59.0
		SD	13.5	15.7	15.9	19.0	21.0	20.1
		SEM	4.5	5.1	4.8	5.1	4.7	5.2
	Form F	M	27.9	32.7	34.5	38.4	56.7	57.9
		SD	13.0	14.6	15.1	18.2	21.2	19.1
		SEM	4.4	4.8	4.6	4.9	4.8	5.0

			Grades					
			9	10	11	12	13	14
Comprehension		n	410	438	386	339	165	74
		r	.75	.76	.76	.82	.77	.81
	Form E	M	15.4	17.1	17.6	19.3	23.3	25.7
		SD	6.7	6.8	6.9	7.4	6.2	5.6
		SEM	3.3	3.3	3.4	3.1	3.0	2.4
	Form F	M	15.5	17.5	18.3	20.0	24.5	26.6
		SD	6.8	7.0	7.3	7.6	6.6	6.0
		SEM	3.4	3.4	3.6	3.2	3.1	2.6
Total		n	408	437	386	339	165	74
		r	.88	.89	.89	.93	.93	.93
	Form E	M	58.4	67.1	69.6	77.5	102.3	110.4
		SD	25.2	27.4	27.8	31.9	31.4	28.5
		SEM	8.7	9.1	9.1	8.5	8.1	7.7
	Form F	M	58.9	67.7	71.1	78.3	105.7	111.2
		SD	24.8	26.5	27.5	31.3	31.9	28.3
		SEM	8.6	8.8	9.0	8.4	8.2	7.6
Reading Rate		n	373	341	360	283	164	72
		r	.62	.62	.67	.76	.71	.82
	Form E	M	231.5	247.6	235.5	235.7	271.9	294.1
		SD	105.4	119.5	98.8	84.5	89.3	86.6
		SEM	64.9	73.2	57.0	41.4	47.8	37.2
	Form F	M	217.1	231.6	233.4	225.8	287.7	294.6
		SD	99.4	109.2	99.4	90.3	107.1	103.5
		SEM	61.2	66.9	57.4	44.2	57.3	44.4

Conclusions

The *Nelson-Denny* is an academically based, rigorous vocabulary and reading comprehension test for high school and college level students. Samples of high school students are fairly representative by region and by socioeconomic level. The college sample is representative of colleges by size, with some over-representation of smaller colleges. There seems regionally to be a higher participation rate of four-year students in the Midwest and a thinning of the Far West two- and particularly four-year samples.

Although the student sample was not selected on the basis of race or ethnic identity, percentages by race indicated that blacks and hispanics are somewhat under represented, especially at the four-year level. Although an effective screening instrument, the predictive use of the test for those students who are college-bound is inadequately supported by the data. The authors' suggestion of a cut-off point (a score below the 35th percentile) used to place incoming college students for remedial or developmental reading programs appears to have been somewhat arbitrarily set.

As a diagnostic tool this test is also limited. The vocabulary breakdown of those words containing prefixes is of some help since good students will use prefixes to identify the meaning of words with which they are unfamiliar. But the test lacks the more sophisticated breakdown used by some of the exclusively diagnostic tests which analyze items by the type of skill required and the content.

The high level of the reading materials (ranging from the 9th to the 16th grade level as measured by the Corrected Dale-Chall formula) combined with the academic nature of the reading comprehension passages and vocabulary, bias this test in favor of the traditional academic-track student. It is not surprising that the Nelson-Denny is a good predictor of performance for college students; the content resembles certain parts of the SAT test to which it has a fairly high statistical correlation.

The difficulty level of this test makes it less than suitable for the high risk student. For example, the lower range of students entering two- or four-year colleges with marginal reading skills (the authors cite a 5th grade level as the lowest level the test was designed to serve [Examiner's manual p. 12]) would find the test very difficult and the content different from the materials they may have encountered in high school or in vocational coursework. In addition, the comprehension passages cover academic content that seems to be somewhat dated, being taken from texts developed in the 60s and 70s.

Some students may also be intimidated by the format which closely resembles the achievement tests regularly used in the kindergarten through twelfth grade.

Placing students into science, mathematics, or vocational programs based on their performance on the *Nelson-Denny* raises a content validity issue. If students do well on the academic material in the *Nelson-Denny Test*, will they do equally well on content which is substantially different? The research suggests that students who perform well on academic reading will also perform well in specific content areas. For students who are marginal, performance will depend much more on their background knowledge of the particular content area (Sticht, 1987). Students scoring below the 35 percentile on the *Nelson-Denny* will need specific assessment and remediation within the content areas of their high school or college courses.

Although the authors have found this test to be a good predictor of college achievement for black students, the norming data make it unclear as to how minority groups perform on this test in relation to their mainstream counterparts. Nonmainstream students might find this test biased towards those with a familiarity of European culture and history. Finally, the Reading Rate subtest is rather superficial and simplistic. Rate is closely related to the difficulty level of the material and familiarity with the content. One trial paragraph is unlikely to be a good measure. This weakness is reflected in the lower reliability quotient of this subtest.

References

Brown, J. I.; Bennett, J. M.; and Hanna, G. (1981). *The Nelson-Denny Reading Test, examiner's manual.* Chicago, IL: Riverside Publishing Co.

Sticht, T. G. (1987). *Functional context education.* San Diego, CA: Applied Behavioral and Cognitive Sciences, Inc.

SPECIALIZED TESTS

Introduction

Reading specialists and classroom teachers are often interested in factors related to the reading process which are not dealt with directly in most reading assessment tests. Included are such factors as listening vocabulary, spelling ability, concepts about print (e.g., knowing what a word or sentence is, left to right orientation, where to start reading in a book), and how the student is performing in other school subjects.

Since these factors may be measured by both formal and informal procedures, it is difficult to establish a set of questions to guide the examiner in the selection of such instruments. Thus, one may generally be concerned about two fundamental issues:

1. What are the correlates or factors of reading success according to the examiner's belief system about the reading process?
2. How are these correlates or factors best assessed?

Once these issues have been addressed and instruments or procedures selected, then standard questions previously listed for norm- and criterion-referenced tests apply. It is this kind of information which helps the examiner to complete the student's reading profile.

Concepts about Print Test

Author: Marie M. Clay

Publisher: Heinemann Publishers

Edition: Third

Copyright: 1985

Reviewer: Betty S. Heathington, University of Tennessee

General Description

The *Concepts about Print Test*, by Marie M. Clay, is included as part of a diagnostic survey in the third edition of Clay's book, *The Early Detection of Reading Difficulties*. The diagnostic survey also includes letter identification, word tests, other reading tests, and writing.

Twenty-four items are used in the *Concepts about Print Test* to probe the print awareness of young children. The test may be classified as a readiness measure to be used to understand a young child's basic understanding of printed language. It may be used to assess fundamental confusions a child may have concerning print.

Procedures for administering, scoring, and interpreting the test are provided. Separate, soft-cover test booklets, entitled *Sand* and *Stones*, are used with the descriptive material in the book.

☐ Basic Format

With a child, the test examiner uses one of the test booklets, *Sand* or *Stones*, saying "I'm going to read you this story but I want you to help me." The examiner then proceeds to question the child concerning aspects of print awareness as the story is read.

For each of the twenty-four items on the test, the examiner is provided with three types of information: (1) an explanation of the concept that is being tested; (2) the exact wording to say to the child; and (3) the scoring requirement for the item.

☐ Intended Use

Clay's intended use of the entire diagnostic survey is for assessment after a child has received instruction for one year. She believes strongly that such an assessment is necessary to plan interventions for those children who are experiencing difficulty.

The *Concepts about Print Test* is to be used by classroom teachers. In her book, Clay provides both the assessment and recovery procedures for use by classroom teachers.

□ Subtests or Test Components

Each of the 24 items on the test serves to assess a separate concept about print. As the examiner reads *Sand* or *Stones* to the child, the 24 items are assessed. The concepts include:

Front of Book. The child is asked to show the examiner the front of the book.

Print Not Picture Carries Message. The child must show where the examiner is to start reading, recognizing that the printed text carries the message, not the picture.

Directional Rule (Where to Start). The child must point to the beginning word to show where the examiner is to start reading the printed text.

Directional Rule (Left to Right). The child must show the examiner which way to go after the first word, recognizing that print is read left to right.

Directional Rule (Return Sweep). The child must show that after reading the first line, the examiner must make a return sweep to the next line, beginning at the left again.

Word by Word Pointing. The child must point to the text, word by word, as the examiner reads slowly.

First and Last Part of Story. The child must indicate to the examiner the location of the first and last parts of the story. A correct response is scored if the child can show first and last with respect to the whole text or a line, word, or letter.

Inversion of Picture. On one page, the picture is printed upside-down: the child is asked to show the bottom of the picture. The child must either explain that the picture must be turned around or must actually turn the book around.

Response to Inverted Print. After correcting for the inverted picture, the child must then decide where reading is to begin and which way to go.

Line Sequence. The child sees two pages of print, a left page and a right page, and must verbalize that the left page of print must be read before the right page.

Word Sequence. On one page in the text booklet, some words are not sequenced correctly. The child is asked to explain what is wrong on the page.

Letter Order. Letters in some words are not sequenced correctly on another page. The child is asked to explain what is wrong on the page.

Re-ordering Letters Within a Word. Letters are incorrectly ordered in several words on a page. The child must notice that letters are incorrectly ordered within a word.

Meaning of Question Mark, Full Stop, Comma, and Quotation Marks. The child must explain the purpose of the question mark, the period, the comma, and quotation marks on the page.

Capital and Lower-Case Correspondence. After the examiner points to a certain capital letter, the child must find a lower-case letter on the page like the capital letter.

Reversible Words. After the examiner reads the page, the child must point to the words "was" and "no".

Letter Concepts. The child must use two cards to block letters on a page. For example, the child must block all letters except one on the page; then the child must block all except two letters.

Word Concepts. Continuing to use the two cards, the child must block all except one word; then the child must block all except two words.

First and Last Letter Concepts. The child must use the two cards to show the first letter of a word and then the last letter of a word.

Capital Letter Concepts. The last task the child must perform is to show the examiner a capital letter on the page.

Technical Aspects

While some research data are provided concerning normalized scores and stanine groups, Clay states that the greatest value of the *Concepts about Print* test is its diagnostic aspects. Its value is in diagnosing whether or not a child understands printed language or whether there is some confusion about how printed language works.

Brief research data are presented concerning the validity and reliability of the test on one of the charts in the book.

☐ Validity

Validity was calculated by correlating the *Concepts about Print* test with word reading for 100 six-year-old children in New Zealand in 1966. There was a correlation of .79 between the two tests.

☐ Reliability

Reliability was checked with 40 urban children in New Zealand, ages five to seven years, in 1968. A .95 KR–20 was obtained.

In 1978, 56 kindergarten children in Texas were tested. Test–retest reliability coefficients of .73 to .89 and corrected split-half coefficients of .84 to .88 were found.

☐ Test Development

Morris and Henderson (1981, p. 279) state that Clay's work with the print concept test is "pioneering descriptive research." The work spans over 20 years of effort by Clay with much of her early work describing the reading development of 100 New Zealand first-graders.

She states that her research question in 1962 was "Can we see the process of learning to read going wrong, close to the onset of reading instruction?" (Clay, 1979). In 1972, she described for teachers some of the results of her research, including the *Concepts About Print Test.* In 1979, she revised and expanded her work, adding a second test booklet, *Stones,* to the print awareness material. The second test booklet can be used with children who are overly familiar with the first test booklet, *Sand.*

In 1976, Clay's research efforts were expanded to developing teaching procedures (recovery procedures) that could be used with children who had been diagnosed as having problems. Her assessments and recovery procedures are intended for classroom teachers. She stresses that teachers must be careful observers of their students' responses to print.

☐ Other Pertinent Data

The test, available in English, has been translated and used with Danish and Spanish speaking children. Clay indicates that the check on concepts about print can be done quickly (5 to 10 minutes). She also believes it can stand alone as a measure of reading readiness or reading progress.

Conclusions

Clay's work with print awareness truly is a pioneering effort. The approach to reading readiness is unlike most readiness tests. Because this test uses an actual book for the assessment and the examiner reads the book to the child, it departs from traditional pencil and paper readiness tests.

☐ Advantages

The test is comprehensive in its assessment of print awareness concepts. The 24 items on the test are fairly discrete in assessing the various aspects of printed language with which children must be aware before they move into further reading instruction.

The test has an automatic validity because it uses reading materials and an actual reading situation to assess print concepts. This is a strength of the test that makes it especially appealing to educators who believe that testing must be as similar to "real" conditions as possible.

A test of print awareness is needed. Teachers need to be able to determine any basic confusions children may have about print before they proceed to other reading instruction. These basic confusions, if not overcome, will affect all other aspects of the child's learning to read. The *Concepts About Print Test* offers teachers a way to make important decisions about the child's facility with print before the child is exposed to expanded instruction.

The test is not a complicated one. The instructions are easy to understand; the procedures are specific. Any classroom teacher should be able to administer the test and interpret the results.

☐ Disadvantages

Because the test must be administered on a one-to-one basis, it will take time for the teacher to administer it to all children in the classroom. However, it is a brief test and the teacher should be able to manage the testing of all children in the classroom in a reasonable period of time.

Information about validity and reliability data is limited. However, because the value of the test is in its diagnostic or criterion assessment, this is not a serious limitation. Because the test is directed at such an important area, print awareness, research data are of interest. Certainly, many researchers will find research using this test an important part of their work. Findings from their work should be included by Clay in her information about the print awareness test.

The *Concepts About Print Test* is worthy of being packaged separately, having its own separate set of instructions, procedures, booklets, and other materials as a unit apart from the entire book. Separate packaging would make the test easier to manage in the classroom.

The test should be a vital part of the early assessment of children's progress in reading. Teachers can use it as a check point of a child's understanding of print. The *Concepts About Print Test* offers untapped possibilities for further research and study.

References

Clay, M. M. (1979). *The early detection of reading difficulties.* (2nd ed.). Auckland, New Zealand: Heinemann Educational Books.

Clay, M. M. (1985). *The early detection of reading difficulties.* (3rd ed.). Auckland, New Zealand: Heinemann Educational Books.

Morris, D., and Henderson, S. H. (1981). Assessing the beginning reader's concept of word. *Reading World* 20, 279–85.

Kaufman Test of Educational Achievement, Brief Form*

Authors: Alan S. Kaufman and Nadeen L. Kaufman

Publisher: American Guidance Service

Copyright: 1985

Reviewers: Robert B. Cooter, Jr., Bowling Green State University
D. Ray Reutzel, Brigham Young University

The *Kaufman Test of Educational Achievement* (K–TEA) is a recently developed, individually administered test of children's school achievement in grades 1 through 12. The Brief Form of the K–TEA is for quick classroom assessment, while the Comprehensive Form is available for clinical assessments. Both forms yield norm-referenced scores in reading, mathematics, and spelling. Because of its potential utility for classroom teachers, this review will focus on the Brief Form of the K–TEA.

Content and Structure of the Test

The K–TEA materials are similar in format to the popular Peabody Individual Achievement Test (Dunn, 1970) which is also published by the American Guidance Service. It includes (1) a very thorough and easy to understand manual providing information on administration, scoring, standardization, validation, and interpretation; (2) one easel-kit containing the items for all three subtests; and (3) individual test protocols (25).

The K–TEA is composed of 52 items for each of the reading and mathematics subtests and 40 spelling subtest items. Of the 52 items presented on the mathematics subtest, the first 25 are computational problems in a paper and pencil format, with the remainder centering on more complex types of applications skills (e.g., story problems, reading graphs, geometry). Similarly, the reading subtest begins with a combination of letter and word identification items followed by a comprehension assessment, all items together totaling 52.

The first four items of the reading subtest are letter identification (T, B, i, a). If the subject were unable to identify those letters, then the examiner would assume that letter knowledge is incomplete and move on to the next subtest. The next 19 items of the reading subtest pertain to word identification, and the final 29 items assess comprehension.

---

* Reprinted with permission from Lance M. Gentile (Ed.), *Reading Psychology* 7(3) 1986.

A rather unique approach to testing reading comprehension has been employed by the authors. Students are requested to respond either orally or gesturally to commands given in printed statements. For example, one item says "show me how you would drink a glass of water." Another item asks the student to pretend to "toss a tennis ball in the air with your left hand and hit it with a racket held in your right hand."

The spelling subtest is a steeply graded list of words that is presented in a typical classroom fashion. The teacher reads the word aloud, uses it in a sentence, then the student either writes the word or spells it orally.

The K–TEA provides an individual test record for noting student responses and for profiling scores on each subtest. For each of the three subtests, the individual test record presents raw scores, standard scores, percentiles, composite scores, subtest comparisons, and a column for "other data." A minor problem with the profile is that it does not include space for noting grade equivalents and stanines, both of which are provided in the tables.

Two useful features of the profile are the descriptive category and subtest comparisons. The descriptive category is a translation of the subtest data into language that is comprehensible to both parents and teachers (i.e., well below average, above average, etc.). Similarly, the subtest comparisons sections allow teachers to determine whether or not differences between subtests are significant.

☐ Administration, Scoring and Interpretation

The easel format of the K–TEA easily lends itself to face to face testing. Subtests are organized in the easel to match the test record. A helpful innovation of the K-TEA is the "remember" page which lists reminders for administering the scoring items on each subtest. The remember page also includes a box giving the suggested starting item for each grade level.

Items in each subtest are grouped in "units" of usually five or more. When the student misses every item in one unit, testing is discontinued. This "discontinue rule" apparently constitutes attainment of the student's ceiling level, although the manual is rather vague regarding the concept of ceiling level.

Once the discontinue rule has been satisfied, the raw scores are derived by subtracting errors from the ceiling or uppermost item. The teacher is then ready to translate these raw scores into norm and interpretive data. Some 139 pages of tables are provided for the translation and may prove to be cumbersome and perhaps overwhelming for many classroom teachers. The publishers have been quite successful in developing quick and easy microcomputer software for scoring such tests as the *Woodcock Reading Mastery Tests* (another difficult test to score) and would be well advised to do the same for the K–TEA.

☐ Test Development and Standardization

Many items included on the K–TEA were taken directly from the Kaufman Assessment Battery for Children (K–ABC), an intelligence test recently developed by the authors of both tests. The reading subtest in particular has nearly 42 percent of its items taken or adapted closely from the K–ABC. The authors state that K–TEA development began in 1981 and ended in 1985 "with the thorough analysis of data from almost 3,000 cases tested..." (Kaufman and Kaufman, 1985, p. 85). While the claim of 3,000 test cases sounds impressive, closer reading reveals that the bulk of testing was with the longer Comprehensive Form, and that the actual number in the national testing program for the Brief Form amounted to 582 students at 27 test sites in 16 states. This is far less than the 1,756 children tested with the new Diagnostic Achievement Battery (Lewandowski, 1985), or the 2,889 cases used in norming the Peabody Individual Achievement Test (Dunn, 1970). Nevertheless, the procedures used in the K–TEA content and item analyses appear to be adequate based on the data presented.

Most geographical regions in the United States were represented, with the exception of the Northwest. Selection of students based on sex, racial or ethnic group, and parental education levels are equivalent with national percentages. However, sample sizes for minority groups are often so low that the reliability of the instrument for minority students must be called into question. For example, only four black students were part of the 11th- and 12-grade samples.

The largest sample of black students on any level was 14 for grade six. Hispanic students were represented even less than blacks with a low of one student at grade ten, and a high of five students at grade twelve. The manual fails to address this issue and somewhat deceptively presents data relevant only to the Comprehensive Form that is far more complimentary. When one considers the small sample sizes used in deriving norms for minority students, the reliability of the data must be considered questionable.

☐ Reliability and Validity

Reliability figures are carefully obtained and acceptable. The K–TEA Brief Form was administered twice to 153 students spread "about equally across the grade range of 1 to 12" (Kaufman and Kaufman, 1985, p. 114) to obtain test–retest reliabilities.

The test–retest coefficients for the separate subtests ranged from .84 (Reading) to .90 (Spelling) for grades 1-6, and clustered at .84 and .85 for all three subtests at the secondary grade levels. The standard error of measurement (SEM) was from two to four points across the age range and about three to five points across the grade range.

Anastasi's (1984) multi-stage approach to determining test validity was applied to the K–TEA Brief Form. This procedure provides some indication of content validity in part answering the question "does the test match the school's curriculum?" The authors indicate that their studies regarding content, construct, and concurrent validity are favorable.

The concurrent validity correlations with reading subtests of the Wide Range Achievement Test and the Peabody Individual Achievement Test were a median r of .62 and .80 respectively. In summary, the statistical properties of the test appear to be acceptable, but may be called into question regarding minority students, as noted previously.

Discussion and Conclusions

The K–TEA is a norm-referenced, individually administered test of academic achievement in reading, mathematics, and spelling for grades 1-12. It seems likely that many educators would find the K–TEA useful as a gross screening instrument when quantitative data are needed.

The manual has been carefully developed and provides many useful tips in test administration. Measurement properties of the K–TEA are competently provided and are essentially acceptable. However, the obtained measurement data should be viewed as suspect with regard to minority students until a more representative norming sample is provided for ascertaining the K–TEA's mensuration properties.

There seem to be two major weaknesses with the K–TEA's reading subtest. First, the letter/word identification and comprehension data are not reported separately on the test record, thus limiting the usefulness of these data. Second, another troublesome aspect of this subtest relates to its organization. Because letter/word identification precedes comprehension, a child could reach his ceiling prior to the comprehension items (24 and 52) thereby providing an estimated reading level based solely on letter and word identification.

The authors do not offer a clear rationale for the selection of the three domains assessed by the K–TEA. When compared to the Peabody Individual Achievement Test (PIAT [Dunn, 1970]), or the new Diagnostic Achievement Battery (DAB [Newcomer and Curtis, 1984]), the K–TEA appears to be something less than comprehensive. The authors strongly suggest the use of their intelligence test, the *Kaufman Assessment Battery for Children* (K–ABC), for a more complete evaluation. However, this would seem to defeat the purpose of a "brief" assessment.

As a quick and relatively reliable gross screening instrument providing both age and grade norms, the K–TEA represents a useful alternative to the WRAT and the PIAT. Whether or not it will become the preferred individually administered achievement test for use in screening, research, and comprehensive testing batteries is yet to be determined by teachers themselves.

References

Anastasi, A. (1984). The K-ABC in historical and contemporary perspective. *Journal of Special Education* 18, 357–66.

Dunn, L. M., and Markwardt, F. (1970). *Peabody Individual Achievement Test*. Circle Pines, MN: American Guidance Service.

Jastak, J. F., and Jastak, S. D. (1978). *Wide Range Achievement Test*. Wilmington, DE: Jastak Associates.

Kaufman, A. S., and Kaufman, N. L. (1985). *Manual for the Kaufman Test of Educational Achievement, Brief Form*. Circle Pines, MN: American Guidance Service.

Lewandowski, L. J. (1985). Test review: Diagnostic achievement battery. *The Reading Teacher* 39, 306–09.

Newcomer, P. L., and Curtis, D. (1984). *Diagnostic Achievement Battery*. Austin, TX: PRO-ED.

Woodcock R. W. (1973). *Woodcock Reading Mastery Tests*. Circle Pines, MN: American Guidance Service.

Peabody Picture Vocabulary Test–Revised (PPVT-R)

Authors: Lloyd M. Dunn and Leota M. Dunn

Publisher: American Guidance Service

Edition: Second

Copyright: 1981

Reviewer: Leo W. Pauls, Emporia State University

General Description
☐ Basic Format

The *Peabody Picture Vocabulary Test–Revised* (PPVT–R) is an individually administered, norm-referenced test of hearing vocabulary. It is available in two forms—L and M.

Each of the two forms contains 175 items in a sequence of increasing difficulty preceded by five sample items. Each of the 175 items contains four black and white illustrations. The examinee is to select the illustration which best depicts the meaning of a stimulus word given orally by the examiner. Items which are too easy or too hard are not administered; consequently, the administration takes only 10 to 20 minutes.

☐ Intended Use

The PPVT–R is intended for individuals two and one-half through 40 years of age. The persons taking the test must be able to generally understand Standard American English and see and hear reasonably well.

☐ Description of Test Components

The major components of the PPVT–R are (1) the manual, (2) an individual test record, (3) a separate series of plates for Form L and Form M bound in an easel-book, and (4) a technical supplement.

Chronological age guides are given in the individual test record to establish an appropriate starting point. Then, through testing, both a basal level and a ceiling level are set. The basal level is the highest eight consecutive correct responses and the ceiling level is the lowest eight consecutive responses containing six errors. The ceiling level minus errors made by the examinee determines the raw score. The raw score can be converted to a standard score, percentile rank, stanine, and age equivalent score.

Technical Aspects

☐ Development

The Peabody Picture Vocabulary Test–Revised was developed during a four-year period of time, 1976 to 1980, with the first two years used for planning and refinement of the items. Through a very thorough and detailed process a pool of 684 words was identified for item tryout. Of the 684 old and new words, 180 were meant for the preschool level (ages two and one half through five), 204 for the intermediate level (ages 5–10), and 300 words for the advanced level (ages 10 through adult). The item tryout process was a four stage procedure with the involvement of 9,099 subjects. A traditional item analysis and the Rasch-Wright model of item analysis were used to select the 350 words for Forms L and M—175 plates per form. Only 111 of the 350 words were used in the original PPVT edition.

The standardization process involved 4,200 children and young people ages 2 years, 6 months through 18 years, 11 months, and 828 adults ages 19 through 40. The subjects in both samples were selected from four United States geographic regions: Northeast, South, North Central, and West. A concerted effort was made to incorporate various parental occupations, different size communities, and a balance between the sexes.

The index used for socioeconomic status was parental occupation. The five identified categories were (1) professional, technical, managers, and administrators; (2) skilled workers and supervisors; (3) operatives and service workers;

(4) sales workers; and (5) laborers, farm supervisors, farmers, and farm managers. The three types of communities used were (1) central cities (50,000 or more population); (2) small towns or suburbs (2,500 to 49,999); and (3) rural areas (less than 2,500 people). The racial configuration closely matched the 1970 census and each age group had 100 females and 100 males.

The actual sample was selected by an identified coordinator in each of the 25 selected communities. This coordinator nominated public, parochial, private, day-care, and preschools which were then contacted by American Guidance Service for possible inclusion in the standardization process.

The norming of the results to determine standard scores, percentile ranks, stanines, and grade percentile ranks was completed immediately after the sampling. Various cross-checks were performed to ensure an accurate set of norms.

□ Reliability

The three methods used to determine the reliability of the PPVT–R were: (1) split-half, (2) immediate retest, and (3) delayed retest.

For the two and one half through 18 year sample, split-half reliabilities showed a range of .67 to .88 for Form L, and .61 to .86 for Form M. For adults the range was .80 to .83.

The immediate retest method for the single age groups yielded reliability coefficients ranging from .73 to .91. For separate grade groups the range was from .64 to .92.

The delayed retest study produced coefficients for raw scores for single age groups to be from .50 to .90 and for single grades to be from .47 to .91. Table 7 summarizes these results.

Table 7 Reliability Coefficients						
	Split-Half		Immediate Retest		Delayed Retest	
	2.5-18	Adults	Single age	Single grade	Single age	Single grade
Correlation coefficients	.61–.88	.80–.83	.73–.91	.64–.92	.50–.90	.47–.91

□ Validity

A study to determine validity of the PPVT–R also used the original PPVT, the Short-Form Test of Academic Aptitude, and the California Achievement Test.

Correlations between the PPVT and the PPVT–R with the Short Form Test of Academic Aptitude provided evidence of the comparative construct validity. In most cases it yielded a higher correlation for the PPVT–R.

Correlations between the PPVT and PPVT–R with the California Achievement Test provided comparative criterion-related predictive validity. Even though most differences did not reach statistical significance, generally the PPVT–R correlated better with the California Achievement Test than did the original PPVT.

Conclusions

The Peabody Picture Vocabulary Test–Revised seems to be a well-designed, well-tested, and easily administered instrument with significant improvements made from the earlier edition. The fact that it took four years to do the revisions along with the addition of many new words are indications of the improvements.

The sampling done of children and young people had a more accurate representation of the populations of the four United States regions than did the sampling of adults. Also, only six states (Iowa, Minnesota, New Mexico, New York, Texas, and Wisconsin) were used for the adult sampling while approximately 21 states were used for the sampling of ages two and one half through 18 years.

As with all tests, one should closely adhere to the directions in the administration of the test and in the interpretation of results.

References

Carvajal, H., et al. (1987). Relationships among scores on the Stanford-Binet IV, Peabody Picture Vocabulary Test-Revised, and Columbia Mental Maturity Scale. *Bulletin of the Psychonomic Society* 25 (4), 275–76.

Mitchell, J. (ed.) (1983). *Tests in Print III*. Lincoln, NE: The University of Nebraska Press.

Robertson, G., and Eisenberg, J. (1981). *Technical supplement for the Peabody Picture Vocabulary Test–Revised*. Circle Pines, MN: American Guidance Service.

Woodcock-Johnson Psycho-Educational Battery

Authors: Richard W. Woodcock and M. Bonner Johnson

Publisher: DLM Teaching Resources

Edition: First

Copyright: 1977

Reviewer: Leo M. Schell, Kansas State University

General Description

This battery consists of three individually administered standardized tests, one each for cognitive ability, scholastic achievement, and interest. It is called a wide-age-range test because it can be used from ages 3 to 80.

It was designed for a variety of users, primarily school psychologists, guidance counselors, speech and language clinicians, etc. It is rarely used by reading teachers, e.g., Chapter I, although it is used extensively in special education, particularly in learning disabilities (LD).

The complete set of materials is quite extensive. The tests are contained in two books, each of which stands as a flip-page easel for ease of administration. There are also two examiner's manuals, a technical manual, and individual response booklets.

It is a relatively simple test to administer and score. To accommodate the wide age range of examinees, items are arranged in order of difficulty. In administering these subtests, a basal level is determined by five consecutive correct items and testing is halted when the ceiling level—five consecutive incorrect items—is reached.

The individual record booklet is well-organized and makes recording results quick and easy.

To help an examiner prepare to give the test, there are guidelines, checklists, and even a practice exercise.

In the three tests, there are a total of 27 subtests. This review will focus on only the tests most pertinent to reading instruction.

Part One: Tests of Cognitive Ability. Consists of 12 subtests ranging in complexity of mental processing from visual matching to concept formation. It requires approximately one hour to administer; however, all subtests need not be given and selective testing is possible. Moreover, a brief scale can be obtained by administering only two tests, Quantitative Concepts and Antonyms–Synonyms.

Of particular interest in this review is that a Reading Aptitude score can be obtained by administering four subtests. Such a score could be used as an expectation measure, similar in use to, but far more accurate than, the potential level obtained via listening on an informal reading inventory (IRI). This indication of expected achievement could be compared with a reader's actual achievement to determine the presence and/or amount of a learning deficit.

Part Two: Tests of Achievement. Consists of ten subtests of which three can be valuable in assessing and/or diagnosing reading achievement. These are Letter–Word Identification, Word Attack, and Passage Comprehension.

Letter–Word Identification requires examinees to identify letters and words. Words are in order of frequency in written language but difficulty of correct pronunciation was also a criterion. (The last word is *puisne*, pronounced pūnē!) Meanings of the words are not measured.

Word Attack requires examinees to apply phonic and structural analysis skills to pronounce nonsense words such as jox, mibgus, and mafreatsun.

The Passage Comprehension subtest departs significantly from most conventional measures of reading comprehension. It uses a modified cloze procedure in which examinees supply only a single missing key word, no matter the level of difficulty or complexity of the language. The most frequently occurring wrong answers are listed in the examiner's manual. And, for some items, questions to elicit another response are supplied should an examinee give a response that is neither clearly right nor clearly wrong.

Individual scores are not provided for each of these subtests. Rather, the three scores are combined into a single composite Reading Cluster score in an attempt to minimize overinterpretation. Reading achievement is thus defined as a broad, multifaceted task. This procedure also results in higher validity for the resulting score.

Part Three: Tests of Interest Level. Consists of five subtests assessing an examinee's degree of preference for participating in different types of activities—scholastic and nonscholastic. These five subtests are Reading, Mathematics, Written Language, Physical, and Social. Any one or any combination of subtests may be given.

The test uses a quite valid procedure of forced-choice, although it may be unexpected by many examiners. Examinees are presented with two activities and asked to choose the one they would rather do. Each subtest consists of 25 forced-choice items.

These tests are usually not administered below grade five but may be given as low as grade three. And, if an examinee has any difficulty with reading, the examiner reads the items aloud.

Most psychologists would consider the Reading Interest subtest misnamed as it measures attitude rather than interest. That is, it indicates how strongly examinees feel toward the reading act rather than indicating topics they are interested in reading about.

The Written Language scale appears to be a valid measure of the examinee's preference for written activities. It could provide valuable information for teachers interested in combining reading and writing instruction.

Even though the subtests are easy to administer and score, the same cannot be said of interpreting the results. Eleven different derived scores are provided, e.g., grade- and age-equivalent scores, percentile ranks, instructional range, and Relative Performance Index.

The grade equivalent and age equivalent scores are just what their names suggest and are easily interpretable. Psychometricians have repeatedly warned educators not to assume that a grade equivalent score indicates level of readability in the same way the instructional level of an IRI does. The technical manual deals with this issue and concludes that, because of this battery's different construction, "the grade equivalent scores derived from it are more likely to represent the level of task difficulty that the subject can perform." This argument seems to have some merit. However, the grade equivalent score needs to be used cautiously.

Two scores merit a reading teacher's attention, instructional range and Relative Performance Index. The instructional range provides two grade equivalent scores, e.g., 2.2 to 3.2. The lower score represents a level of instruction that probably would be perceived by the examinee as easy (the independent reading level) whereas the higher one represents the level that probably would be perceived by the examinee as difficult (the frustration reading level).

The Relative Performance Index (RPI) is too complicated to discuss here in detail, but, essentially, it predicts how well the examinee could be expected to perform on tasks similar to the ones tested. It is a variation of the relative mastery scores used in the *Woodcock Reading Mastery Tests* and uses 90 percent as the level of mastery. An RPI of 70/90 would mean that the examinee could be expected to demonstrate 70 percent mastery with those tests on which the reference group performed with 90 percent mastery. Thus, an RPI of 90/90 would be average, 99/90 superior, and anything below 82/90 would be considered below average.

The assumptions and statistical calculations underlying these scores are quite complex and even debatable. Users should study the manual thoroughly and try to comprehend the meaning of these scores before interpreting them. The response book is so admirably arranged to facilitate recording that interpretation appears equally simple and straightforward. Such may not be the case. Caution in interpretation is in order.

Technical Aspects

☐ Test Development and Norming

Test development is far more important in wide-age-range tests than in ones for homogeneous groups because each item needs to be of a specified level of difficulty, something like steps in relation to other items. The assumptions, models, and mathematics are highly complex—and difficult to meet. The degree to which they are not met makes the test's scores that much less precise. Information in the technical manual is both impressive and spotty. Users can have general confidence in the scores' precision, but should interpret them with some degree of caution.

The norming sample is also very important because validity of the test's norms depends upon how representative is the norming sample of the population with whom the examinee's test results are to be compared. All reasonable care seems to have been exercised in this regard, particularly with regard for race and sex—even if the procedure for weighting the subtests was quite tricky.

☐ Validity

No direct evidence is presented to substantiate content validity, an estimate of the extent to which items are representative of the curriculum and of psychological processes involved in reading. The authors state only that the items were developed with the assistance of "outside experts" and experienced teachers.

Concurrent validity, or how effective a test is compared with similar tests, is difficult to find support using evidence presented by the authors. While some attempt is made to compare the WRMT–R with the *Woodcock-Johnson Reading Tests*, one must ultimately conclude that they are not truly independent criterion measures. Since satisfactory evidence of concurrent validity is limited, users are left to decide for themselves the relative value of these tests.

☐ Reliability

Both the Reading Aptitude and the Reading Achievement reliability coefficients are quite high—in the mid .90s—indicating that users can feel that scores are quite accurate and that nearly the same results would occur if the tests were given again.

The standard error of measurement is fairly small, indicating that users should not expect much error to be present in an obtained score, that the obtained score will not vary greatly from the "true score." The subtest profile on the response booklet is particularly helpful with standard error because there is a filled band indicating the probable range within which the examinee's true score occurred. A more valid picture is thus given than if only a point were marked on a line.

Conclusions

The reading parts of the Woodcock-Johnson (W-J) battery have many desirable qualities and uses that should be valuable in clinical situations, e.g., resource rooms, or where individual testing is feasible. The wide-age-range attribute is one of the most obvious of these. Teachers beyond the elementary school level—including those of post-high school students—should find it quite valuable as there are few decent tests for this age group.

However, in administering the test to several high school and college students, a definite ceiling effect was found. Several students "topped out," i.e., they did not miss five consecutive items. The test may be most appropriate for older students who are poor readers.

As repeatedly mentioned in this review, scores should be interpreted cautiously, certainly more so than scores from standardized group silent reading tests. Not only is the matter of scaling and weighting items and scores complicated and tricky—and subject to considerable error—but the reading score seems weighted toward word pronunciation and away from what most of us view as reading comprehension. The *Iowa Tests of Basic Skills* (ITBS) with which this battery was correlated to determine its validity is designed to require a high degree of thought by examinees. The reading score of the W-J battery correlated only between .76 to .81 with the ITBS indicating that the two tests only partly measure the same thing. My belief is that a large part of this difference is due to the lack of comprehension required in the W-J's reading score.

A complicating factor is the modified cloze format used to measure reading comprehension. It measures syntactical-semantic factors at the literal level but the degree to which it taps higher level comprehension is unknown.

The Reading and the Written Language Interest scales are useful because virtually no measures of these traits are available—particularly for post-elementary school students. They can provide some important information typically unavailable or not collected for post-elementary school students. However, a significant caveat needs to be made which is not mentioned in the examiner's manual. It is extremely easy for examinees to fake "correct" responses, i.e., the one most aligned with the examiner's value system. Examinees need to be asked to respond truthfully and insightfully.

Overall, if more reading teachers were familiar with this battery and had it available, they would probably discover valuable uses for at least parts of it. It certainly merits examination, and possibly use, despite its less-than-perfect nature.

TEST SUMMARY CHART

Test	Type of Adminis-tration	Time for Adminis-tration (approx., in minutes)	Validity Evidence	Reliability	Norming Data	Alter-nate Forms
INFORMAL READING INVENTORIES (IRI)						
ARI	Individual	30	Satisfactory	NE	NP	Yes
Bader	Individual	60	NE	NE	NP	Yes
CRI	Individual	20	NE	NE	NP	Yes
DRS	Individual	45	Satisfactory	Acceptable	Poor	Yes
Ekwall	Individual	30	NE	NE	NE	Yes
Burns/Roe	Individual	20	NE	NE	NE	Yes
RMI	Individual	30	NE	NE	NE	N/A
Sucher/ Allred	Group	40	Satisfactory	Acceptable	Minimal	Yes
DIAGNOSTIC READING TESTS						
Brigance	Individual	90	Fair	NE	Minimal	Yes
DST	Individual	30	Satisfactory	Acceptable	Excellent	No
Durrel	Individual	90	Fair	Acceptable	Fair/poor	No
Gates/ McKillop	Individual	30	NE	Incomplete	Poor	No
WRMT–R	Individual	45	Satisfactory	Acceptable	Excellent	Yes

Test	Type of Adminis- tration	Time for Adminis- tration (approx., in minutes)	Validity Evidence	Reliability	Norming Data	Alter- nate Forms
GROUP READING TESTS						
Gates/ MacGinitie	Group	70-105	Satisfactory	Acceptable	Excellent	Yes
MAT–6	Group	120	Fair	Acceptable	Excellent	Yes
SDRT	Group	105-120	Fair/poor	Acceptable	Excellent	Yes
ADULT READING TESTS						
DRP	Group	30	Satisfactory	Acceptable	Good	NA
TABE	Individual		Satisfactory	Acceptable	Fair	Yes
N–D RT	Group	60	Fair	Acceptable	Fair	Yes
SPECIALIZED TESTS						
Concepts about Print	Individual	15	Fair	Acceptable	Fair	Yes
K–TEA	Individual	30	Satisfactory	Acceptable	Good	No
PPVT–R	Individual	15	Fair	Acceptable	Good	Yes
W–J	Individual	120	Satisfactory	Acceptable	Good	Yes

RATING SCALES AND KEY

NA = Not applicable
NE = Not established
NP = Not provided with test materials

Ratings for validity: Poor, Fair, Satisfactory
Ratings for reliability: NE, Incomplete, Poor, Acceptable
Ratings for Norming Data: NE, Minimal, Poor, Fair, Good, Excellent

GLOSSARY

Acuity the physical ability of a person to see and hear.

Affective measurements assessments which have to do with the reader's interests, attitudes, and motivations. By identifying students' affective dimensions, teachers are presumably better able to match reading materials to reader interest.

Battery a group of assessment tests and procedures used to analyze a student's relative reading abilities, needs, and interests.

Concurrent validity a determination of how accurately a given test is able to deliver comparable information with other known and respected tests thought to be similar. In other words, if a new informal reading inventory (IRI) is introduced, a reading researcher may wish to compare results obtained using the new IRI with results obtained using the *Classroom Reading Inventory* with the same sample students. Results of this comparison may be used to establish concurrent validity.

Construct validity a determination of how meaningful test scores may be in light of current theories about the reading act. For example, one may reasonably ask, "Are reading test scores meaningful if they fail to consider the affective domain?" The central question for all validity matters should be, "Does this test measure what it claims to measure?" If it fails to measure all known and measurable elements, then appropriate steps must be taken to complete the assessment program.

Content validity how well a test measures what the student has been taught. Not only is it considered prudent for test makers to plan tests carefully to reflect a balanced sampling of the curriculum that has been taught, but also to make sure that the format of the test items themselves match the kind of examples used in the classroom to model and evaluate skills. Important court cases in Florida and elsewhere have given great weight to the notion of content validity in making educational decisions. Content validity is also known as *curricular validity.*

Criterion-referenced test a test designed to measure whether a student is capable of performing a given reading behavior. This usually means that the student is able to perform the task at a predetermined proficiency level, thus the term *criterion.*

Diagnostic test/assessment a test which measures isolated reading skills. The underlying assumption with these types of measures is that reading is an act which may be taken apart and the various pieces measured. The parts of the diagnostic test used to measure separate reading components are called *subtests.* This type of measurement is considered the antithesis of holistic assessment.

Face validity this concept suggests that the overall appearance of the test is important, especially to those untrained in educational assessment. For example, if a reading specialist or classroom teacher is interested in purchasing an informal reading inventory he or she will expect it to look like other IRIs he or she has seen. If a new IRI does not have the expected features, say sight word lists and graded passages, then she may well reject the new IRI (even if the new test is actually more attuned to advances in reading research). Obviously, face validity is not a particularly scientific or scholarly concept.

Functional reading levels reading ability levels usually identified using an informal reading inventory. They are called the independent (easy), instructional, and frustration (failure) reading levels. Occasionally a version of these labels are used with other types of tests, as with the *Woodcock Reading Mastery Tests–Revised.*

Grade equivalent one way of expressing a test score indicating the grade level (and months in a grade) at which the average person in a norm group sample had a given number correct. Thus, a grade equivalent score of 4.7 means that the student made the same score as the average student in the normative sample who was in the seventh month of the fourth grade. Note that this does not necessarily indicate that the student is reading at the mid-fourth grade level.

Group test a test designed to be given to more than one student at a time by one examiner.

Individual test a test that may be given to only one student at a time.

Norm-referenced test a test that has been standardized using a cross section of students from around the country who represent the various demographics from each geographic region. This allows a student's performance on the test to be compared to the "norm group" so that relative ability may be determined.

Percentile rank   another way of expressing test scores using a norm-referenced measure indicating the percent of students that scored above or below a given point. For example, if a student had a percentile ranking of 55 on a word identification subtest, then that student's performance was higher than 55 percent of students in the norm group.

Raw score   the number of correct items on a test.

Reliability   an indication of how consistently a test can measure a given skill. In other words, if a test is given to a student today and then administered again a week from today, the test score should be the same, or nearly the same, if the conditions are similar. Reliability of tests (norm referenced) are reported using a *reliability coefficient.* The reliability coefficient is a mathematical calculation which is reported statistically with a range of -1.00 to +1.00. A reliability coefficient near +1.00 has a very positive or high reliability, while coefficients dipping below about +.75 are generally considered unreliable. For norm referenced measures, .75 or better is generally thought to be an acceptable reliability for subtests, and .90 or better is considered a desirable range for total or overall test reliability.

Standard error of measurement   a statistical point value that indicates how much random error should be expected when administering a norm-referenced test. This number is calculated along with the raw score so that a true score range can be determined. For example, if a student has a raw score of 45 and the standard error of measurement is plus or minus 3 score points, then the student's true score will most likely fall somewhere between 42 and 48 inclusive (68 percent of the time). Standard error of measurement is often abbreviated SEm, Smeas, or SEmeas.

Stanine   a method of expressing test scores which divides the total possible range of scores into nine equal parts, with one being the lowest performance level and nine the highest. The word stanine comes from the expression standard nine and is based on the normal curve.

Validity   an explanation of how well a test measures what it claims to measure. For example, a reading test is theoretically designed to measure students' reading ability. To the extent that a reading test measures important aspects of reading ability it purports to measure it is valid. There are several types of validity. *See also* Concurrent validity, Construct validity, Content validity, and Face validity.

ISBN 0-89787-527-3